RefTeX User Manual

A catalogue record for this book is available from the Hong Kong Public Libraries.

Published in Hong Kong by Samurai Media Limited.

Email: info@samuraimedia.org

ISBN 978-988-8381-62-3

1 Introduction

RefTeX is a specialized package for support of labels, references, citations, and the index in LaTeX. RefTeX wraps itself round four LaTeX macros: `\label`, `\ref`, `\cite`, and `\index`. Using these macros usually requires looking up different parts of the document and searching through BibTeX database files. RefTeX automates these time-consuming tasks almost entirely. It also provides functions to display the structure of a document and to move around in this structure quickly.

Don't be discouraged by the size of this manual, which covers RefTeX in great depth. All you need to know to use RefTeX can be summarized on two pages (see Section 1.2 [RefTeX in a Nutshell], page 3). You can go back later to other parts of this document when needed.

See Section 7.10 [Imprint], page 43, for information about who to contact for help, bug reports or suggestions.

1.1 Installation

RefTeX has been bundled and pre-installed with Emacs since version 20.2. It has also been bundled and pre-installed with XEmacs 19.16–20.x. XEmacs 21.x users want to install the corresponding plug-in package which is available from the XEmacs FTP site. See the XEmacs 21.x documentation on package installation for details.

Users of earlier Emacs distributions (including Emacs 19) or people craving for new features and bugs can get a copy of the RefTeX distribution from the maintainer's web page. See Section 7.10 [Imprint], page 43, for more information. The following instructions will guide you through the process of installing such a distribution.

1.1.1 Building and Installing

Note: Currently installation is supported for Emacs only. XEmacs users might want to refer to the RefTeX package available through the package system of XEmacs.

Installation with make

In order to install RefTeX, unpack the distribution and edit the header of the Makefile. Basically, you need to change the path specifications for Emacs Lisp files and info files. Also, enter the name of your Emacs executable (usually either 'emacs' or 'xemacs').

Then, type

```
make
make install
```

to compile and install the code and documentation.

Per default RefTeX is installed in its own subdirectory which might not be on your load path. In this case, add it to load path with a command like the following, replacing the sample directory with the one where RefTeX is installed in your case.

```
(add-to-list 'load-path "/path/to/reftex")
```

Put this command into your init file before other RefTeX-related settings.

Installation by Hand

If you want to get your hands dirty, there is also the possibility to install by manually copying files.

a. Copy the reftex*.el lisp files to a directory on your load path. Make sure that no old copy of RefTeX shadows these files.

b. Byte compile the files. The sequence of compiling should be: reftex-var.el, reftex.el, and then all the others.

c. Copy the info file reftex.info to the info directory.

1.1.2 Loading RefTeX

In order to make the most important functions for entering RefTeX mode available add the following line to your init file.

```
(require 'reftex)
```

1.1.3 Entering RefTeX Mode

To turn RefTeX Mode on and off in a particular buffer, use *M-x reftex-mode RET*. To turn on RefTeX Mode for all LaTeX files, add the following lines to your '.emacs' file:

```
(add-hook 'LaTeX-mode-hook 'turn-on-reftex)    ; with AUCTeX LaTeX mode
(add-hook 'latex-mode-hook 'turn-on-reftex)    ; with Emacs latex mode
```

That's all!

To get started, read the documentation, in particular the summary. (see Section 1.2 [RefTeX in a Nutshell], page 3)

In order to produce a printed version of the documentation, use `make pdf` to produce a reftex.pdf file. Analogously you can use the `dvi`, `ps`, or `html` targets to create DVI, PostScript or HTML files.

1.1.4 Environment

RefTeX needs to access all files which are part of a multifile document, and the BibTeX database files requested by the `\bibliography` command. To find these files, RefTeX will require a search path, i.e. a list of directories to check. Normally this list is stored in the environment variables `TEXINPUTS` and `BIBINPUTS` which are also used by RefTeX. However, on some systems these variables do not contain the full search path. If RefTeX does not work for you because it cannot find some files, See Section 7.6 [Finding Files], page 35.

1.2 RefTEX in a Nutshell

1. **Table of Contents**
   Typing `C-c =` (reftex-toc) will show a table of contents of the document. This buffer can display sections, labels and index entries defined in the document. From the buffer, you can jump quickly to every part of your document. Press *?* to get help.

2. **Labels and References**
   RefTEX helps to create unique labels and to find the correct key for references quickly. It distinguishes labels for different environments, knows about all standard environments (and many others), and can be configured to recognize any additional labeled environments you have defined yourself (variable `reftex-label-alist`).

   - **Creating Labels**
     Type `C-c (` (reftex-label) to insert a label at point. RefTEX will either
     - derive a label from context (default for section labels)
     - prompt for a label string (default for figures and tables) or
     - insert a simple label made of a prefix and a number (all other environments)

     Which labels are created how is configurable with the variable `reftex-insert-label-flags`.

   - **Referencing Labels**
     To make a reference, type `C-c )` (reftex-reference). This shows an outline of the document with all labels of a certain type (figure, equation,...) and some label context. Selecting a label inserts a `\ref{label}` macro into the original buffer.

3. **Citations**
   Typing `C-c [` (reftex-citation) will let you specify a regular expression to search in current BibTEX database files (as specified in the `\bibliography` command) and pull out a list of matches for you to choose from. The list is *formatted* and sorted. The selected article is referenced as '`\cite{key}`' (see the variable `reftex-cite-format` if you want to insert different macros).

4. **Index Support**
   RefTEX helps to enter index entries. It also compiles all entries into an alphabetically sorted '`*Index*`' buffer which you can use to check and edit the entries. RefTEX knows about the standard index macros and can be configured to recognize any additional macros you have defined (`reftex-index-macros`). Multiple indices are supported.

   - **Creating Index Entries**
     To index the current selection or the word at point, type `C-c /` (reftex-index-selection-or-word). The default macro `reftex-index-default-macro` will be used. For a more complex entry type `C-c <` (reftex-index), select any of the index macros and enter the arguments with completion.

   - **The Index Phrases File (Delayed Indexing)**
     Type `C-c \` (reftex-index-phrase-selection-or-word) to add the current word or selection to a special *index phrase file*. RefTEX can later search the document for occurrences of these phrases and let you interactively index the matches.

   - **Displaying and Editing the Index**
     To display the compiled index in a special buffer, type `C-c >` (reftex-display-index). From that buffer you can check and edit all entries.

5. **Viewing Cross-References**

When point is on the *key* argument of a cross-referencing macro (\label, \ref, \cite, \bibitem, \index, and variations) or inside a BibTEX database entry, you can press *C-c &* (reftex-view-crossref) to display corresponding locations in the document and associated BibTEX database files.

When the enclosing macro is \cite or \ref and no other message occupies the echo area, information about the citation or label will automatically be displayed in the echo area.

6. **Multifile Documents**

Multifile Documents are fully supported. The included files must have a file variable TeX-master or tex-main-file pointing to the master file. RefTEX provides cross-referencing information from all parts of the document, and across document borders ('xr.sty').

7. **Document Parsing**

RefTEX needs to parse the document in order to find labels and other information. It does it automatically once and updates its list internally when reftex-label and reftex-index are used. To enforce reparsing, call any of the commands described above with a raw *C-u* prefix, or press the *r* key in the label selection buffer, the table of contents buffer, or the index buffer.

8. **AUCTEX**

If your major LATEX mode is AUCTEX, RefTEX can cooperate with it (see variable reftex-plug-into-AUCTeX). AUCTEX contains style files which trigger appropriate settings in RefTEX, so that for many of the popular LATEX packages no additional customizations will be necessary.

9. **Useful Settings**

To integrate RefTeX with AUCTEX, use

```
(setq reftex-plug-into-AUCTeX t)
```

To make your own LATEX macro definitions known to RefTEX, customize the variables

reftex-label-alist	(for label macros/environments)
reftex-section-levels	(for sectioning commands)
reftex-cite-format	(for \cite-like macros)
reftex-index-macros	(for \index-like macros)
reftex-index-default-macro	(to set the default macro)

If you have a large number of macros defined, you may want to write an AUCTEX style file to support them with both AUCTEX and RefTEX.

10. **Where Next?**

Go ahead and use RefTEX. Use its menus until you have picked up the key bindings. For an overview of what you can do in each of the different special buffers, press *?*. Read the manual if you get stuck, or if you are curious what else might be available. The first part of the manual explains in a tutorial way how to use and customize RefTEX. The second part is a command and variable reference.

2 Table of Contents

Pressing the keys *C-c =* pops up a buffer showing the table of contents of the document. By default, this '*toc*' buffer shows only the sections of a document. Using the *l* and *i* keys you can display all labels and index entries defined in the document as well.

With the cursor in any of the lines denoting a location in the document, simple key strokes will display the corresponding part in another window, jump to that location, or perform other actions.

Here is a list of special commands in the '*toc*' buffer. A summary of this information is always available by pressing *?*.

General

?	Display a summary of commands.
0-9, -	Prefix argument.

Moving around

n	Goto next entry in the table of contents.
p	Goto previous entry in the table of contents.
C-c C-n	Goto next section heading. Useful when many labels and index entries separate section headings.
C-c C-p	Goto previous section heading.
N z	Jump to section N, using the prefix arg. For example, *3 z* jumps to section 3.

Access to document locations

SPC	Show the corresponding location in another window. This command does *not* select that other window.
TAB	Goto the location in another window.
RET	Go to the location and hide the '*toc*' buffer. This will restore the window configuration before `reftex-toc` (*C-c =*) was called.
mouse-2	Clicking with mouse button 2 on a line has the same effect as RET. See also variable `reftex-highlight-selection`, Section 9.10 [Options (Fontification)], page 65.
f	Toggle follow mode. When follow mode is active, the other window will always show the location corresponding to the line at point in the '*toc*' buffer. This is similar to pressing SPC after each cursor motion. The default for this flag can be set with the variable `reftex-toc-follow-mode`. Note that only context in files already visited is shown. RefTeX will not visit a file just for follow mode. See, however, the variable `reftex-revisit-to-follow`.
.	Show calling point in another window. This is the point from where `reftex-toc` was last called.

Promotion and Demotion

<   Promote the current section. This will convert \section to \chapter, \subsection to \section etc. If there is an active region, all sections in the region will be promoted, including the one at point. To avoid mistakes, RefTeX requires a fresh document scan before executing this command – if necessary, it will automatically do this scan and ask the user to repeat the promotion command.

>   Demote the current section. This is the opposite of promotion. It will convert \chapter to \section etc. If there is an active region, all sections in the region will be demoted, including the one at point.

M-%   Rename the label at point. While generally not recommended, this can be useful when a package like 'fancyref' is used where the label prefix determines the wording of a reference. After a promotion/demotion it may be necessary to change a few labels from 'sec:xyz' to 'cha:xyz' or vice versa. This command can be used to do this - it launches a query replace to rename the definition and all references of a label.

Exiting

q   Hide the '*toc*' buffer, return to the position where reftex-toc was last called.

k   Kill the '*toc*' buffer, return to the position where reftex-toc was last called.

C-c >   Switch to the '*Index*' buffer of this document. With prefix '2', restrict the index to the section at point in the '*toc*' buffer.

Controlling what gets displayed

t   Change the maximum level of toc entries displayed in the '*toc*' buffer. Without prefix arg, all levels will be included. With prefix arg (e.g 3 t), ignore all toc entries with level greater than *arg* (3 in this case). Chapters are level 1, sections are level 2. The mode line 'T<>' indicator shows the current value. The default depth can be configured with the variable reftex-toc-max-level.

F   Toggle the display of the file borders of a multifile document in the '*toc*' buffer. The default for this flag can be set with the variable reftex-toc-include-file-boundaries.

l   Toggle the display of labels in the '*toc*' buffer. The default for this flag can be set with the variable reftex-toc-include-labels. When called with a prefix argument, RefTeX will prompt for a label type and include only labels of the selected type in the '*toc*' buffer. The mode line 'L<>' indicator shows which labels are included.

i   Toggle the display of index entries in the '*toc*' buffer. The default for this flag can be set with the variable reftex-toc-include-index-entries. When called with a prefix argument, RefTeX will prompt for a specific index and include only entries in the selected index in the '*toc*' buffer. The mode line 'I<>' indicator shows which index is used.

c   Toggle the display of label and index context in the '*toc*' buffer. The default for this flag can be set with the variable reftex-toc-include-context.

Updating the buffer

g   Rebuild the '*toc*' buffer. This does *not* rescan the document.

r   Reparse the LaTeX document and rebuild the '*toc*' buffer. When `reftex-enable-partial-scans` is non-`nil`, rescan only the file this location is defined in, not the entire document.

C-u r   Reparse the *entire* LaTeX document and rebuild the '*toc*' buffer.

x   Switch to the '*toc*' buffer of an external document. When the current document is using the `xr` package (see Section 3.7 [xr (LaTeX package)], page 19), RefTeX will switch to one of the external documents.

Automatic recentering

d   Toggle the display of a dedicated frame displaying just the '*toc*' buffer. Follow mode and visiting locations will not work that frame, but automatic recentering will make this frame always show your current editing location in the document (see below).

a   Toggle the automatic recentering of the '*toc*' buffer. When this option is on, moving around in the document will cause the '*toc*' to always highlight the current section. By default, this option is active while the dedicated '*TOC*' frame exists. See also the variable `reftex-auto-recenter-toc`.

In order to define additional commands for the '*toc*' buffer, the keymap `reftex-toc-map` may be used.

If you call `reftex-toc` while the '*toc*' buffer already exists, the cursor will immediately jump to the right place, i.e. the section from which `reftex-toc` was called will be highlighted. The command *C-c -* (`reftex-toc-recenter`) will only redisplay the '*toc*' buffer and highlight the correct line without actually selecting the '*toc*' window. This can be useful to quickly find out where in the document you currently are. You can also automate this by asking RefTeX to keep track of your current editing position in the TOC. The TOC window will then be updated whenever you stop typing for more than `reftex-idle-time` seconds. By default this works only with the dedicated '*TOC*' frame. But you can also force automatic recentering of the TOC window on the current frame with

        (setq reftex-auto-recenter-toc t)

The section macros recognized by RefTeX are all LaTeX section macros (from `\part` to `\subsubparagraph`) and the commands `\addchap` and `\addsec` from the KOMA-Script classes. Additional macros can be configured with the variable `reftex-section-levels`. It is also possible to add certain LaTeX environments to the table of contents. This is probably only useful for theorem-like environments. See Section 3.4 [Defining Label Environments], page 12, for an example.

3 Labels and References

LaTeX provides a powerful mechanism to deal with cross-references in a document. When writing a document, any part of it can be marked with a label, like '\label{mark}'. LaTeX records the current value of a certain counter when a label is defined. Later references to this label (like '\ref{mark}') will produce the recorded value of the counter.

Labels can be used to mark sections, figures, tables, equations, footnotes, items in enumerate lists etc. LaTeX is context sensitive in doing this: A label defined in a figure environment automatically records the figure counter, not the section counter.

Several different environments can share a common counter and therefore a common label category. For example labels in both **equation** and **eqnarray** environments record the value of the same counter – the equation counter.

3.1 Creating Labels

In order to create a label in a LaTeX document, press *C-c (* (**reftex-label**). Just like LaTeX, RefTeX is context sensitive and will figure out the environment it currently is in and adapt the label to that environment. A label usually consists of a short prefix indicating the type of the label and a unique mark. RefTeX has three different modes to create this mark.

1. A label can be derived from context. This means, RefTeX takes the context of the label definition and constructs a label from that[1]. This works best for section labels, where the section heading is used to construct a label. In fact, RefTeX's default settings use this method only for section labels. You will be asked to confirm the derived label, or edit it.

2. We may also use a simple unique number to identify a label. This is mostly useful for labels where it is difficult to come up with a very good descriptive name. RefTeX's default settings use this method for equations, enumerate items and footnotes. The author of RefTeX tends to write documents with many equations and finds it impossible to come up with good names for each of them. These simple labels are inserted without query, and are therefore very fast. Good descriptive names are not really necessary as RefTeX will provide context to reference a label (see Section 3.2 [Referencing Labels], page 9).

3. The third method is to ask the user for a label. This is most useful for things which are easy to describe briefly and do not turn up too frequently in a document. RefTeX uses this for figures and tables. Of course, one can enter the label directly by typing the full '\label{mark}'. The advantage of using **reftex-label** anyway is that RefTeX will know that a new label has been defined. It will then not be necessary to rescan the document in order to access this label later.

If you want to change the way certain labels are created, check out the variable **reftex-insert-label-flags** (see Section 9.3 [Options (Creating Labels)], page 52).

---

[1] Note that the context may contain constructs which are invalid in labels. RefTeX will therefore strip the accent from accented Latin-1 characters and remove everything else which is not valid in labels. This mechanism is safe, but may not be satisfactory for non-western languages. Check the following variables if you need to change things: **reftex-translate-to-ascii-function**, **reftex-derive-label-parameters**, **reftex-label-illegal-re**, **reftex-abbrev-parameters**.

If you are using AUCTeX to write your LaTeX documents, you can set it up to delegate the creation of labels to RefTeX. See Section 7.8 [AUCTeX], page 37, for more information.

3.2 Referencing Labels

RefTeX scans the document in order to find all labels. To make referencing labels easier, it assigns to each label a category, the *label type* (for example section, table, figure, equation, etc.). In order to determine the label type, RefTeX parses around each label to see in what kind of environments it is located. You can speed up the parsing by using type-specific prefixes for labels and configuring the variable `reftex-trust-label-prefix`.

Referencing Labels is really at the heart of RefTeX. Press `C-c )` in order to reference a label (`reftex-reference`). This will start a selection process and finally insert the complete '`\ref{label}`' into the buffer.

First, you can select which reference macro you want to use, e.g. '`\ref`' or '`\pageref`'. Later in the process you have another chance to make this selection and you can therefore disable this step by customizing `reftex-ref-macro-prompt` if you find it too intrusive. See Section 3.6 [Reference Styles], page 18.

Then, RefTeX will determine the label category which is required. Often that can be figured out from context. For example, if you write '`As shown in eq.`' and then press `C-c )`, RefTeX knows that an equation label is going to be referenced. If it cannot figure out what label category is needed, it will query for one.

You will then be presented with a label selection menu. This is a special buffer which contains an outline of the document along with all labels of the given label category. In addition, next to the label there will be one line of context of the label definition, which is some text in the buffer near the label definition. Usually this is sufficient to identify the label. If you are unsure about a certain label, pressing SPC will show the label definition point in another window.

In order to reference a label, move the cursor to the correct label and press RET. You can also reference several labels with a single call to `reftex-reference` by marking entries with the *m* key (see below).

Here is a list of special commands in the selection buffer. A summary of this information is always available from the selection process by pressing *?*.

General

?	Show a summary of available commands.
0-9,-	Prefix argument.

Moving around

n	Go to next label.
p	Go to previous label.
b	Jump back to the position where you last left the selection buffer. Normally this should get you back to the last referenced label.
C-c C-n	Goto next section heading.
C-c C-p	Goto previous section heading.

N z   Jump to section N, using the prefix arg. For example *3 z* jumps to section 3.

Displaying Context

SPC   Show the surroundings of the definition of the current label in another window. See also the *f* key.

f   Toggle follow mode. When follow mode is active, the other window will always display the full context of the current label. This is similar to pressing SPC after each cursor motion. Note that only context in files already visited is shown. RefTEX will not visit a file just for follow mode. See, however, the variable `reftex-revisit-to-follow`.

.   Show insertion point in another window. This is the point from where you called `reftex-reference`.

Selecting a label and creating the reference

RET   Insert a reference to the label at point into the buffer from which the selection process was started. When entries have been marked, RET references all marked labels.

`mouse-2`   Clicking with mouse button 2 on a label will accept it like RET would. See also variable `reftex-highlight-selection`, Section 9.11 [Options (Misc)], page 67.

`m - + ,`   Mark the current entry. When several entries have been marked, pressing *RET* will accept all of them and place them into several `\ref` macros. The special markers ',-+' also store a separator to be inserted before the corresponding reference. So marking six entries with the keys 'm , , - , +' will give a reference list like this (see the variable `reftex-multiref-punctuation`)

                 In eqs. (1), (2), (3)--(4), (5) and (6)

u   Unmark a marked entry.

a   Accept the marked entries and put all labels as a comma-separated list into one *single* `\ref` macro. Some packages like 'saferef.sty' support multiple references in this way.

l   Use the last referenced label(s) again. This is equivalent to moving to that label and pressing RET.

TAB   Enter a label with completion. This may also be a label which does not yet exist in the document.

v   Cycle forward through active reference macros. The selected macro is displayed by the 'S<...>' indicator in the mode line of the selection buffer. This mechanism comes in handy if you are using LaTeX packages like `varioref` or `fancyref` and want to use the special referencing macros they provide (e.g. `\vref` or `\fref`) instead of `\ref`.

V   Cycle backward through active reference macros.

Exiting

q   Exit the selection process without inserting any reference into the buffer.

Controlling what gets displayed

> The defaults for the following flags can be configured with the variable `reftex-label-menu-flags` (see Section 9.4 [Options (Referencing Labels)], page 53).

c   Toggle the display of the one-line label definition context in the selection buffer.

F   Toggle the display of the file borders of a multifile document in the selection buffer.

t   Toggle the display of the table of contents in the selection buffer. With prefix *arg*, change the maximum level of toc entries displayed to *arg*. Chapters are level 1, sections are level 2.

Toggle the display of a label counter in the selection buffer.

%   Toggle the display of labels hidden in comments in the selection buffers. Sometimes, you may have commented out parts of your document. If these parts contain label definitions, RefTeX can still display and reference these labels.

Updating the buffer

g   Update the menu. This will rebuilt the menu from the internal label list, but not reparse the document (see *r*).

r   Reparse the document to update the information on all labels and rebuild the menu. If the variable `reftex-enable-partial-scans` is non-`nil` and your document is a multifile document, this will reparse only a part of the document (the file in which the label at point was defined).

C-u r   Reparse the *entire* document.

s   Switch the label category. After prompting for another label category, a menu for that category will be shown.

x   Reference a label from an external document. With the LaTeX package `xr` it is possible to reference labels defined in another document. This key will switch to the label menu of an external document and let you select a label from there (see Section 3.7 [xr], page 19).

In order to define additional commands for the selection process, the keymap `reftex-select-label-map` may be used.

3.3 Builtin Label Environments

RefTeX needs to be aware of the environments which can be referenced with a label (i.e. which carry their own counters). By default, RefTeX recognizes all labeled environments and macros discussed in *The LaTeX Companion by Goossens, Mittelbach & Samarin, Addison-Wesley 1994.*. These are:

- `figure`, `figure*`, `table`, `table*`, `equation`, `eqnarray`, `enumerate`, the `\footnote` macro (this is the LaTeX core stuff)

- `align`, `gather`, `multline`, `flalign`, `alignat`, `xalignat`, `xxalignat`, `subequations` (from AMS-LaTeX's `amsmath.sty` package)

- the `\endnote` macro (from `endnotes.sty`)

- `Beqnarray` (`fancybox.sty`)

- `floatingfig` ('`floatfig.sty`')
- `longtable` ('`longtable.sty`')
- `figwindow`, `tabwindow` ('`picinpar.sty`')
- `SCfigure`, `SCtable` ('`sidecap.sty`')
- `sidewaysfigure`, `sidewaystable` ('`rotating.sty`')
- `subfigure`, `subfigure*`, the `\subfigure` macro ('`subfigure.sty`')
- `supertabular` ('`supertab.sty`')
- `wrapfigure` ('`wrapfig.sty`')

If you want to use other labeled environments, defined with `\newtheorem`, RefTeX needs to be configured to recognize them (see Section 3.4 [Defining Label Environments], page 12).

3.4 Defining Label Environments

RefTeX can be configured to recognize additional labeled environments and macros. This is done with the variable `reftex-label-alist` (see Section 9.2 [Options (Defining Label Environments)], page 48). If you are not familiar with Lisp, you can use the `custom` library to configure this rather complex variable. To do this, use

```
M-x customize-variable RET reftex-label-alist RET
```

Here we will discuss a few examples, in order to make things clearer. It can also be instructive to look at the constant `reftex-label-alist-builtin` which contains the entries for all the builtin environments and macros (see Section 3.3 [Builtin Label Environments], page 11).

3.4.1 Theorem and Axiom Environments

Suppose you are using `\newtheorem` in LaTeX in order to define two new environments, `theorem` and `axiom`

```
\newtheorem{axiom}{Axiom}
\newtheorem{theorem}{Theorem}
```

to be used like this:

```
\begin{axiom}
\label{ax:first}
   ....
\end{axiom}
```

So we need to tell RefTeX that `theorem` and `axiom` are new labeled environments which define their own label categories. We can either use Lisp to do this (e.g. in '`.emacs`') or use the custom library. With Lisp it would look like this

```
(setq reftex-label-alist
   '(("axiom"   ?a "ax:" "~\\ref{%s}" nil ("axiom"   "ax.") -2)
     ("theorem" ?h "thr:" "~\\ref{%s}" t   ("theorem" "th.") -3)))
```

The type indicator characters `?a` and `?h` are used for prompts when RefTeX queries for a label type. `?h` was chosen for `theorem` since `?t` is already taken by `table`. Note that also `?s`, `?f`, `?e`, `?i`, `?n` are already used for standard environments.

The labels for Axioms and Theorems will have the prefixes '`ax:`' and '`thr:`', respectively. See Section 7.8 [AUCTeX], page 37, for information on how AUCTeX can use RefTeX to automatically create labels when a new environment is inserted into a buffer. Additionally, the following needs to be added to one's .emacs file before AUCTEX will automatically create labels for the new environments.

```
(add-hook 'LaTeX-mode-hook
    (lambda ()
      (LaTeX-add-environments
        '("axiom" LaTeX-env-label)
        '("theorem" LaTeX-env-label))))
```

The '`~\ref{%s}`' is a format string indicating how to insert references to these labels.

The next item indicates how to grab context of the label definition.

— `t` means to get it from a default location (from the beginning of a `\macro` or after the `\begin` statement). `t` is *not* a good choice for eqnarray and similar environments.

— `nil` means to use the text right after the label definition.

— For more complex ways of getting context, see the variable `reftex-label-alist` (Section 9.2 [Options (Defining Label Environments)], page 48).

The following list of strings is used to guess the correct label type from the word before point when creating a reference. For example if you write: '`As we have shown in Theorem`' and then press `C-c )`, RefTEX will know that you are looking for a theorem label and restrict the menu to only these labels without even asking.

The final item in each entry is the level at which the environment should produce entries in the table of context buffer. If the number is positive, the environment will produce numbered entries (like `\section`), if it is negative the entries will be unnumbered (like `\section*`). Use this only for environments which structure the document similar to sectioning commands. For everything else, omit the item.

To do the same configuration with `customize`, you need to click on the `[INS]` button twice to create two templates and fill them in like this:

```
Reftex Label Alist: [Hide]
[INS] [DEL] Package or Detailed  : [Value Menu] Detailed:
            Environment or \macro : [Value Menu] String: axiom
            Type specification    : [Value Menu] Char  : a
            Label prefix string   : [Value Menu] String: ax:
            Label reference format: [Value Menu] String: ~\ref{%s}
            Context method        : [Value Menu] After label
            Magic words:
              [INS] [DEL] String: axiom
              [INS] [DEL] String: ax.
              [INS]
            [X] Make TOC entry    : [Value Menu] Level: -2
[INS] [DEL] Package or Detailed  : [Value Menu] Detailed:
            Environment or \macro : [Value Menu] String: theorem
            Type specification    : [Value Menu] Char  : h
            Label prefix string   : [Value Menu] String: thr:
            Label reference format: [Value Menu] String: ~\ref{%s}
            Context method        : [Value Menu] Default position
```

```
Magic words:
  [INS] [DEL] String: theorem
  [INS] [DEL] String: theor.
  [INS] [DEL] String: th.
  [INS]
[X] Make TOC entry     : [Value Menu] Level: -3
```

Depending on how you would like the label insertion and selection for the new environments to work, you might want to add the letters 'a' and 'h' to some of the flags in the variables `reftex-insert-label-flags` (see Section 9.3 [Options (Creating Labels)], page 52) and `reftex-label-menu-flags` (see Section 9.4 [Options (Referencing Labels)], page 53).

3.4.2 Quick Equation Macro

Suppose you would like to have a macro for quick equations. It could be defined like this:

```
\newcommand{\quickeq}[1]{\begin{equation} #1 \end{equation}}
```

and used like this:

```
Einstein's equation is \quickeq{E=mc^2 \label{eq:einstein}}.
```

We need to tell RefTEX that any label defined in the argument of the `\quickeq` is an equation label. Here is how to do this with lisp:

```
(setq reftex-label-alist '(("\\quickeq{}" ?e nil nil 1 nil)))
```

The first element in this list is now the macro with empty braces as an *image* of the macro arguments. `?e` indicates that this is an equation label, the different `nil` elements indicate to use the default values for equations. The '1' as the fifth element indicates that the context of the label definition should be the first argument of the macro.

Here is again how this would look in the customization buffer:

```
Reftex Label Alist: [Hide]
[INS] [DEL] Package or Detailed   : [Value Menu] Detailed:
            Environment or \macro : [Value Menu] String: \quickeq{}
            Type specification    : [Value Menu] Char  : e
            Label prefix string   : [Value Menu] Default
            Label reference format: [Value Menu] Default
            Context method        : [Value Menu] Macro arg nr: 1
            Magic words:
              [INS]
            [ ] Make TOC entry    : [Value Menu] No entry
```

3.4.3 Figure Wrapping Macro

Suppose you want to make figures not directly with the figure environment, but with a macro like

```
\newcommand{\myfig}[5][tbp]{%
  \begin{figure}[#1]
    \epsimp[#5]{#2}
    \caption{#3}
    \label{#4}
```

```
\end{figure}}
```
which would be called like
```
\myfig[htp]{filename}{caption text}{label}{1}
```
Now we need to tell RefTEX that the fourth argument of the \myfig macro *is itself* a figure label, and where to find the context.
```
(setq reftex-label-alist
      '(("\\myfig[]{}{}{*}{}" ?f nil nil 3)))
```
The empty pairs of brackets indicate the different arguments of the \myfig macro. The '*' marks the label argument. ?f indicates that this is a figure label which will be listed together with labels from normal figure environments. The nil entries for prefix and reference format mean to use the defaults for figure labels. The '3' for the context method means to grab the third macro argument – the caption.

As a side effect of this configuration, reftex-label will now insert the required naked label (without the \label macro) when point is directly after the opening parenthesis of a \myfig macro argument.

Again, here the configuration in the customization buffer:
```
[INS] [DEL] Package or Detailed   : [Value Menu] Detailed:
            Environment or \macro : [Value Menu] String: \myfig[]{}{}{*}{}
            Type specification    : [Value Menu] Char  : f
            Label prefix string   : [Value Menu] Default
            Label reference format: [Value Menu] Default
            Context method        : [Value Menu] Macro arg nr: 3
            Magic words:
              [INS]
            [ ] Make TOC entry     : [Value Menu] No entry
```

3.4.4 Adding Magic Words

Sometimes you don't want to define a new label environment or macro, but just change the information associated with a label category. Maybe you want to add some magic words, for another language. Changing only the information associated with a label category is done by giving nil for the environment name and then specify the items you want to define. Here is an example which adds German magic words to all predefined label categories.
```
(setq reftex-label-alist
  '((nil ?s nil nil nil ("Kapitel" "Kap." "Abschnitt" "Teil"))
    (nil ?e nil nil nil ("Gleichung" "Gl."))
    (nil ?t nil nil nil ("Tabelle"))
    (nil ?f nil nil nil ("Figur" "Abbildung" "Abb."))
    (nil ?n nil nil nil ("Anmerkung" "Anm."))
    (nil ?i nil nil nil ("Punkt"))))
```

3.4.5 Using \eqref

Another case where one only wants to change the information associated with the label category is to change the macro which is used for referencing the label. When working with the AMS-LATEX, you might prefer \eqref for doing equation references. Here is how to do this:

```
(setq reftex-label-alist '((nil ?e nil "~\\eqref{%s}" nil nil)))
```

RefTEX has also a predefined symbol for this special purpose. The following is equivalent to the line above.

```
(setq reftex-label-alist '(AMSTeX))
```

Note that this is automatically done by the 'amsmath.el' style file of AUCTEX (see Section 7.8.2 [Style Files], page 38) – so if you use AUCTEX, this configuration will not be necessary.

3.4.6 Non-standard Environments

Some LATEX packages define environment-like structures without using the standard '\begin..\end' structure. RefTEX cannot parse these directly, but you can write your own special-purpose parser and use it instead of the name of an environment in an entry for `reftex-label-alist`. The function should check if point is currently in the special environment it was written to detect. If so, it must return a buffer position indicating the start of this environment. The return value must be `nil` on failure to detect the environment. The function is called with one argument *bound*. If non-`nil`, *bound* is a boundary for backwards searches which should be observed. We will discuss two examples.

Some people define abbreviations for environments, like \be for \begin{equation}, and \ee for \end{equation}. The parser function would have to search backward for these macros. When the first match is \ee, point is not in this environment. When the first match is \be, point is in this environment and the function must return the beginning of the match. To avoid scanning too far, we can also look for empty lines which cannot occur inside an equation environment. Here is the setup:

```
;; Setup entry in reftex-label-alist, using all defaults for equations
(setq reftex-label-alist '((detect-be-ee ?e nil nil nil nil)))


(defun detect-be-ee (bound)
  ;; Search backward for the macros or an empty line
  (if (re-search-backward
       "\\(^[ \t]*\n\\)|\\(\\\\ee\\>\\)\\|\\(\\\\be\\>\\)" bound t)
      (if (match-beginning 2)
          (match-beginning 2)    ; Return start of environment
        nil)                      ; Return nil because env is closed
    nil))                         ; Return nil for not found
```

A more complex example is the 'linguex.sty' package which defines list macros '\ex.', '\a.', '\b.' etc. for lists which are terminated by '\z.' or by an empty line.

```
\ex.  \label{ex:12} Some text in an exotic language ...
    \a. \label{ex:13} more stuff
    \b. \label{ex:14} still more stuff
        \a. List on a deeper level
        \b. Another item
        \b. and the third one
    \z.
    \b. Third item on this level.
```

```
... text after the empty line terminating all lists
```

The difficulty is that the '\a.' lists can nest and that an empty line terminates all list levels in one go. So we have to count nesting levels between '\a.' and '\z.'. Here is the implementation for RefTeX.

```
(setq reftex-label-alist
      '((detect-linguex ?x "ex:" "~\\ref{%s}" nil ("Example" "Ex."))))

(defun detect-linguex (bound)
  (let ((cnt 0))
    (catch 'exit
      (while
          ;; Search backward for all possible delimiters
          (re-search-backward
           (concat "\\(^[ \t]*\n\\)\\|\\(\\\\z\\.\\)\\|"
                   "\\(\\ex[ig]?\\.\\)\\|\\(\\\\a\\.\\)")
           nil t)
        ;; Check which delimiter was matched.
        (cond
         ((match-beginning 1)
          ;; empty line terminates all - return nil
          (throw 'exit nil))
         ((match-beginning 2)
          ;; \z. terminates one list level - decrease nesting count
          (decf cnt))
         ((match-beginning 3)
          ;; \ex. : return match unless there was a \z. on this level
          (throw 'exit (if (>= cnt 0) (match-beginning 3) nil)))
         ((match-beginning 4)
          ;; \a. : return match when on level 0, otherwise
          ;;       increment nesting count
          (if (>= cnt 0)
              (throw 'exit (match-beginning 4))
            (incf cnt)))))))))
```

3.4.7 Putting it all together

When you have to put several entries into `reftex-label-alist`, just put them after each other in a list, or create that many templates in the customization buffer. Here is a lisp example which uses several of the entries described above:

```
(setq reftex-label-alist
      '(("axiom"   ?a "ax:"  "~\\ref{%s}" nil ("axiom"   "ax.") -2)
        ("theorem" ?h "thr:" "~\\ref{%s}" t   ("theorem" "theor." "th.") -3)
        ("\\quickeq{}" ?e nil nil 1 nil)
        AMSTeX
        ("\\myfig[]{}{}{*}{}" ?f nil nil 3)
        (detect-linguex ?x "ex:" "~\\ref{%s}" nil ("Example" "Ex."))))
```

3.5 Reference Info

When point is idle for more than `reftex-idle-time` seconds on the argument of a `\ref` macro, the echo area will display some information about the label referenced there. Note that the information is only displayed if the echo area is not occupied by a different message.

RefTeX can also display the label definition corresponding to a `\ref` macro, or all reference locations corresponding to a `\label` macro. See Chapter 6 [Viewing Cross-References], page 32, for more information.

3.6 Reference Styles

In case you defined your own macros for referencing or you are using LaTeX packages providing specialized macros to be used instead of `\ref`, RefTeX provides ways to select and insert them in a convenient way.

RefTeX comes equipped with a set of so-called reference styles where each relates to one or more reference macros. The standard macros '`\ref`' and '`\pageref`' or provided by the "Default" style. The "Varioref" style offers macros for the '`varioref`' LaTeX package ('`\vref`', '`\Vref`', '`\Ref`', '`\vpageref`'), "Fancyref" for the '`fancyref`' package ('`\fref`', '`\Fref`') and "Hyperref" for the '`hyperref`' package ('`\autoref`', '`\autopageref`').

A style can be toggled by selecting the respective entry in the '`Reference Style`' menu. Changes made through the menu will only last for the Emacs session. In order to configure a preference permanently, the variable `reftex-ref-style-default-list` should be customized. This variable specifies the list of styles to be activated. It can also be set as a file variable if the preference should be set for a specific file.

In case the built-in styles do not suffice, you can add additional macros and styles to the variable `reftex-ref-style-alist`. Those do not necessarily have to be related to a certain LaTeX package but can follow an arbitrary grouping rule. For example you could define a style called "Personal" for your personal referencing macros. (When changing the variable you should be aware that other Emacs packages, like AUCTeX, might rely on the entries from the default value to be present.)

Once a style is active the macros it relates to are available for selection when you are about to insert a reference. In general this process involves three steps: the selection of a reference macro, a label type and a label. Reference macros can be chosen in the first and last step.

In the first step you will be presented with a list of macros from which you can select one by typing a single key. If you dislike having an extra step for reference macro selection, you can disable it by customizing `reftex-ref-macro-prompt` and relying only on the selection facilities provided in the last step.

In the last step, i.e. the label selection, two key bindings are provided to set the reference macro. Type V in order to cycle forward through the list of available macros or V to cycle backward. The mode line of the selection buffer shows the macro currently selected.

In case you are not satisfied with the order of macros when cycling through them you should adapt the order of entries in the variable `reftex-ref-style-alist` to fit your liking.

For each entry in `reftex-ref-style-alist` a function with the name `reftex-<package>-<macro>` (e.g. `reftex-varioref-vref`) will be created automatically by RefTeX. These functions can be used instead of *C-c)* and provide an alternative way of having your favorite referencing macro preselected and if cycling through the macros seems inconvenient to you.[2]

In former versions of RefTeX only support for `varioref` and `fancyref` was included. `varioref` is a LaTeX package to create cross-references with page information. `fancyref` is a package where a macro call like `\fref{fig:map-of-germany}` creates not only the number of the referenced counter but also the complete text around it, like 'Figure 3 on the preceding page'. In order to make it work you need to use label prefixes like 'fig:' consistently – something RefTeX does automatically. For each of these packages a variable could be configured to make its macros to take precedence over `\ref`. Those were `reftex-vref-is-default` and `reftex-fref-is-default` respectively. While still working, these variables are deprecated now. Instead of setting them, the variable `reftex-ref-style-default-list` should be adapted now.

3.7 xr: Cross-Document References

The LaTeX package `xr` makes it possible to create references to labels defined in external documents. The preamble of a document using `xr` will contain something like this:

```
\usepackage{xr}
\externaldocument[V1-]{volume1}
\externaldocument[V3-]{volume3}
```

and we can make references to any labels defined in these external documents by using the prefixes 'V1-' and 'V3-', respectively.

RefTeX can be used to create such references as well. Start the referencing process normally, by pressing *C-c)*. Select a label type if necessary. When you see the label selection buffer, pressing *x* will switch to the label selection buffer of one of the external documents. You may then select a label as before and RefTeX will insert it along with the required prefix.

For this kind of inter-document cross-references, saving of parsing information and the use of multiple selection buffers can mean a large speed-up (see Section 7.7 [Optimizations], page 36).

---

[2] You could e.g. bind `reftex-varioref-vref` to *C-c v* and `reftex-fancyref-fref` to *C-c f*.

4 Citations

Citations in LaTeX are done with the \cite macro or variations of it. The argument of the macro is a citation key which identifies an article or book in either a BibTeX database file or in an explicit **thebibliography** environment in the document. RefTeX's support for citations helps to select the correct key quickly.

4.1 Creating Citations

In order to create a citation, press *C-c [*. RefTeX then prompts for a regular expression which will be used to search through the database and present the list of matches to choose from in a selection process similar to that for selecting labels (see Section 3.2 [Referencing Labels], page 9).

The regular expression uses an extended syntax: '&&' defines a logic **and** for regular expressions. For example '**Einstein&&Bose**' will match all articles which mention Bose-Einstein condensation, or which are co-authored by Bose and Einstein. When entering the regular expression, you can complete on known citation keys. RefTeX also offers a default when prompting for a regular expression. This default is the word before the cursor or the word before the current '\cite' command. Sometimes this may be a good search key.

RefTeX prefers to use BibTeX database files specified with a \bibliography macro to collect its information. Just like BibTeX, it will search for the specified files in the current directory and along the path given in the environment variable BIBINPUTS. If you do not use BibTeX, but the document contains an explicit **thebibliography** environment, RefTeX will collect its information from there. Note that in this case the information presented in the selection buffer will just be a copy of relevant \bibitem entries, not the structured listing available with BibTeX database files.

In the selection buffer, the following keys provide special commands. A summary of this information is always available from the selection process by pressing *?*.

General

?   Show a summary of available commands.

0-9,-   Prefix argument.

Moving around

n   Go to next article.

p   Go to previous article.

Access to full database entries

SPC   Show the database entry corresponding to the article at point, in another window. See also the *f* key.

f   Toggle follow mode. When follow mode is active, the other window will always display the full database entry of the current article. This is equivalent to pressing SPC after each cursor motion. With BibTeX entries, follow mode can be rather slow.

Selecting entries and creating the citation

RET   Insert a citation referencing the article at point into the buffer from which the selection process was started.

mouse-2	Clicking with mouse button 2 on a citation will accept it like RET would. See also variable `reftex-highlight-selection`, Section 9.11 [Options (Misc)], page 67.
m	Mark the current entry. When one or several entries are marked, pressing **a** or **A** accepts all marked entries. Also, RET behaves like the **a** key.
u	Unmark a marked entry.
a	Accept all (marked) entries in the selection buffer and create a single \cite macro referring to them.
A	Accept all (marked) entries in the selection buffer and create a separate \cite macro for each of it.
e	Create a new BibTEX database file which contains all *marked* entries in the selection buffer. If no entries are marked, all entries are selected.
E	Create a new BibTEX database file which contains all *unmarked* entries in the selection buffer. If no entries are marked, all entries are selected.
TAB	Enter a citation key with completion. This may also be a key which does not yet exist.
.	Show insertion point in another window. This is the point from where you called `reftex-citation`.

Exiting

q	Exit the selection process without inserting a citation into the buffer.

Updating the buffer

g	Start over with a new regular expression. The full database will be rescanned with the new expression (see also *r*).
r	Refine the current selection with another regular expression. This will *not* rescan the entire database, but just the already selected entries.

In order to define additional commands for this selection process, the keymap `reftex-select-bib-map` may be used.

Note that if you do not use Emacs to edit the BibTEX database files, RefTEX will ask if the related buffers should be updated once it detects that the files were changed externally. If you do not want to be bothered by such queries, you can activate Auto Revert mode for these buffers by adding the following expression to your init file:

```
(add-hook 'bibtex-mode-hook 'turn-on-auto-revert-mode)
```

4.2 Citation Styles

The standard LATEX macro \cite works well with numeric or simple key citations. To deal with the more complex task of author-year citations as used in many natural sciences, a variety of packages has been developed which define derived forms of the \cite macro. RefTEX can be configured to produce these citation macros as well by setting the variable `reftex-cite-format`. For the most commonly used LATEX packages (`natbib`, `harvard`, `chicago`, `jurabib`) and for ConTEXt this may be done from the menu, under `Ref->Citation Styles`.

Since there are usually several macros to create the citations, executing `reftex-citation` (`C-c [`) starts by prompting for the correct macro. For the Natbib style, this looks like this:

```
SELECT A CITATION FORMAT

[^M]    \cite{%l}
[t]     \citet{%l}
[T]     \citet*{%l}
[p]     \citep{%l}
[P]     \citep*{%l}
[e]     \citep[e.g.][]{%l}
[s]     \citep[see][]{%l}
[a]     \citeauthor{%l}
[A]     \citeauthor*{%l}
[y]     \citeyear{%l}
```

If citation formats contain empty pairs of square brackets, RefTeX will prompt for values of these optional arguments if you call the `reftex-citation` command with a `C-u` prefix. Following the most generic of these packages, `natbib`, the builtin citation packages always accept the *t* key for a *textual* citation (like: `Jones et al. (1997) have shown...`) as well as the *p* key for a parenthetical citation (like: `As shown earlier (Jones et al, 1997)`).

To make one of these styles the default, customize the variable `reftex-cite-format` or put into '`.emacs`':

```
(setq reftex-cite-format 'natbib)
```

You can also use AUCTeX style files to automatically set the citation style based on the `usepackage` commands in a given document. See Section 7.8.2 [Style Files], page 38, for information on how to set up the style files correctly.

4.3 Citation Info

When point is idle for more than `reftex-idle-time` seconds on the argument of a `\cite` macro, the echo area will display some information about the article cited there. Note that the information is only displayed if the echo area is not occupied by a different message.

RefTeX can also display the `\bibitem` or BibTeX database entry corresponding to a `\cite` macro, or all citation locations corresponding to a `\bibitem` or BibTeX database entry. See Chapter 6 [Viewing Cross-References], page 32.

4.4 Chapterbib and Bibunits

`chapterbib` and `bibunits` are two LaTeX packages which produce multiple bibliographies in a document. This is no problem for RefTeX as long as all bibliographies use the same BibTeX database files. If they do not, it is best to have each document part in a separate file (as it is required for `chapterbib` anyway). Then RefTeX will still scan the locally relevant databases correctly. If you have multiple bibliographies within a *single file*, this may or may not be the case.

4.5 Citations outside LaTeX

The command `reftex-citation` can also be executed outside a LaTeX buffer. This can be useful to reference articles in the mail buffer and other documents. You should *not* enter `reftex-mode` for this, just execute the command. The list of BibTeX files will in this case be taken from the variable `reftex-default-bibliography`. Setting the variable `reftex-cite-format` to the symbol `locally` does a decent job of putting all relevant information about a citation directly into the buffer. Here is the lisp code to add the *C-c [* binding to the mail buffer. It also provides a local binding for `reftex-cite-format`.

```
(add-hook 'mail-setup-hook
          (lambda () (define-key mail-mode-map "\C-c["
                       (lambda ()
                         (interactive)
                         (let ((reftex-cite-format 'locally))
                           (reftex-citation))))))
```

4.6 Database Subsets

RefTeX offers two ways to create a new BibTeX database file.

The first option produces a file which contains only the entries actually referenced in the current document. This can be useful if the database is only meant for a single document and you want to clean it of old and unused ballast. It can also be useful while writing a document together with collaborators, in order to avoid sending around the entire (possibly very large) database. To create the file, use *M-x reftex-create-bibtex-file*, also available from the menu under `Ref->Global Actions->Create Bibtex File`. The command will prompt for a BibTeX file name and write the extracted entries to that file.

The second option makes use of the selection process started by the command *C-c [* (see Section 4.1 [Creating Citations], page 20). This command uses a regular expression to select entries, and lists them in a formatted selection buffer. After pressing the *e* key (mnemonics: Export), the command will prompt for the name of a new BibTeX file and write the selected entries to that file. You can also first mark some entries in the selection buffer with the *m* key and then export either the *marked* entries (with the *e* key) or the *unmarked* entries (with the *E* key).

5 Index Support

LaTeX has builtin support for creating an Index. The LaTeX core supports two different indices, the standard index and a glossary. With the help of special LaTeX packages ('multind.sty' or 'index.sty'), any number of indices can be supported.

Index entries are created with the `\index{entry}` macro. All entries defined in a document are written out to the '.aux' file. A separate tool must be used to convert this information into a nicely formatted index. Tools used with LaTeX include `MakeIndex` and `xindy`.

Indexing is a very difficult task. It must follow strict conventions to make the index consistent and complete. There are basically two approaches one can follow, and both have their merits.

1. Part of the indexing should already be done with the markup. The document structure should be reflected in the index, so when starting new sections, the basic topics of the section should be indexed. If the document contains definitions, theorems or the like, these should all correspond to appropriate index entries. This part of the index can very well be developed along with the document. Often it is worthwhile to define special purpose macros which define an item and at the same time make an index entry, possibly with special formatting to make the reference page in the index bold or underlined. To make RefTeX support for indexing possible, these special macros must be added to RefTeX's configuration (see Section 5.5 [Defining Index Macros], page 30).

2. The rest of the index is often just a collection of where in the document certain words or phrases are being used. This part is difficult to develop along with the document, because consistent entries for each occurrence are needed and are best selected when the document is ready. RefTeX supports this with an *index phrases file* which collects phrases and helps indexing the phrases globally.

Before you start, you need to make sure that RefTeX knows about the index style being used in the current document. RefTeX has builtin support for the default `\index` and `\glossary` macros. Other LaTeX packages, like the 'multind' or 'index' package, redefine the `\index` macro to have an additional argument, and RefTeX needs to be configured for those. A sufficiently new version of AUCTeX (9.10c or later) will do this automatically. If you really don't use AUCTeX (you should!), this configuration needs to be done by hand with the menu (`Ref->Index Style`), or globally for all your documents with

```
(setq reftex-index-macros '(multind))      or
(setq reftex-index-macros '(index))
```

5.1 Creating Index Entries

In order to index the current selection or the word at the cursor press *C-c /* (`reftex-index-selection-or-word`). This causes the selection or word '*word*' to be replaced with '`\index{word}word`'. The macro which is used (`\index` by default) can be configured with the variable `reftex-index-default-macro`. When the command is called with a prefix argument (*C-u C-c /*), you get a chance to edit the generated index entry. Use this to change the case of the word or to make the entry a subentry, for example by entering '`main!sub!word`'. When called with two raw *C-u* prefixes (*C-u C-u C-c /*), you will be asked for the index macro as well. When there is nothing selected and no word at point, this command will just call `reftex-index`, described below.

In order to create a general index entry, press `C-c <` (`reftex-index`). RefTEX will prompt for one of the available index macros and for its arguments. Completion will be available for the index entry and, if applicable, the index tag. The index tag is a string identifying one of multiple indices. With the 'multind' and 'index' packages, this tag is the first argument to the redefined `\index` macro.

5.2 The Index Phrases File

RefTEX maintains a file in which phrases can be collected for later indexing. The file is located in the same directory as the master file of the document and has the extension '`.rip`' (**R**eftex **I**ndex **P**hrases). You can create or visit the file with `C-c |` (`reftex-index-visit-phrases-buffer`). If the file is empty it is initialized by inserting a file header which contains the definition of the available index macros. This list is initialized from `reftex-index-macros` (see Section 5.5 [Defining Index Macros], page 30). You can edit the header as needed, but if you define new LATEX indexing macros, don't forget to add them to `reftex-index-macros` as well. Here is a phrase file header example:

```
% -*- mode: reftex-index-phrases -*-
%                           Key   Macro Format          Repeat
%------------------------------------------------------------
>>>INDEX_MACRO_DEFINITION:   i     \index{%s}            t
>>>INDEX_MACRO_DEFINITION:   I     \index*{%s}           nil
>>>INDEX_MACRO_DEFINITION:   g     \glossary{%s}         t
>>>INDEX_MACRO_DEFINITION:   n     \index*[name]{%s}     nil
%------------------------------------------------------------
```

The macro definition lines consist of a unique letter identifying a macro, a format string and the *repeat* flag, all separated by TAB. The format string shows how the macro is to be applied, the '`%s`' will be replaced with the index entry. The repeat flag indicates if *word* is indexed by the macro as '`\index{`*word*`}`' (*repeat* = `nil`) or as '`\index{`*word*`}`*word*' (*repeat* = `t`). In the above example it is assumed that the macro `\index*{`*word*`}` already typesets its argument in the text, so that it is unnecessary to repeat *word* outside the macro.

5.2.1 Collecting Phrases

Phrases for indexing can be collected while writing the document. The command `C-c \` (`reftex-index-phrase-selection-or-word`) copies the current selection (if active) or the word near point into the phrases buffer. It then selects this buffer, so that the phrase line can be edited. To return to the LATEX document, press `C-c C-c` (`reftex-index-phrases-save-and-return`).

You can also prepare the list of index phrases in a different way and copy it into the phrases file. For example you might want to start from a word list of the document and remove all words which should not be indexed.

The phrase lines in the phrase buffer must have a specific format. RefTEX will use font-lock to indicate if a line has the proper format. A phrase line looks like this:

```
[key] <TABs> phrase [<TABs> arg[&&arg]... [ || arg]...]
```

<TABs> stands for white space containing at least one TAB. *key* must be at the start of the line and is the character identifying one of the macros defined in the file header. It is optional - when omitted, the first macro definition line in the file will be used for this phrase. The *phrase* is the phrase to be searched for when indexing. It may contain several words separated by spaces. By default the search phrase is also the text entered as argument of the index macro. If you want the index entry to be different from the search phrase, enter another TAB and the index argument *arg*. If you want to have each match produce several index entries, separate the different index arguments with ' && '[1]. If you want to be able to choose at each match between several different index arguments, separate them with ' || '[2]. Here is an example:

```
%-----------------------------------------------------------------
I     Sun
i     Planet       Planets
i     Vega         Stars!Vega
      Jupiter      Planets!Jupiter
i     Mars         Planets!Mars || Gods!Mars || Chocolate Bars!Mars
i     Pluto        Planets!Pluto && Kuiper Belt Objects!Pluto
```

So 'Sun' will be indexed directly as '\index*{Sun}', while 'Planet' will be indexed as '\index{Planets}Planet'. 'Vega' will be indexed as a subitem of 'Stars'. The 'Jupiter' line will also use the 'i' macro as it was the first macro definition in the file header (see above example). At each occurrence of 'Mars' you will be able choose between indexing it as a subitem of 'Planets', 'Gods' or 'Chocolate Bars'. Finally, every occurrence of 'Pluto' will be indexed as '\index{Planets!Pluto}\index{Kuiper Belt Objects!Pluto}Pluto' and will therefore create two different index entries.

5.2.2 Consistency Checks

Before indexing the phrases in the phrases buffer, they should be checked carefully for consistency. A first step is to sort the phrases alphabetically - this is done with the command *C-c C-s* (`reftex-index-sort-phrases`). It will sort all phrases in the buffer alphabetically by search phrase. If you want to group certain phrases and only sort within the groups, insert empty lines between the groups. Sorting will only change the sequence of phrases within each group (see the variable `reftex-index-phrases-sort-in-blocks`).

A useful command is *C-c C-i* (`reftex-index-phrases-info`) which lists information about the phrase at point, including an example of how the index entry will look like and the number of expected matches in the document.

Another important check is to find out if there are double or overlapping entries in the buffer. For example if you are first searching and indexing 'Mars' and then 'Planet Mars', the second phrase will not match because of the index macro inserted before 'Mars' earlier. The command *C-c C-t* (`reftex-index-find-next-conflict-phrase`) finds the next phrase in the buffer which is either duplicate or a subphrase of another phrase. In order to check the whole buffer like this, start at the beginning and execute this command repeatedly.

---

[1] '&&' with optional spaces, see `reftex-index-phrases-logical-and-regexp`.

[2] '||' with optional spaces, see `reftex-index-phrases-logical-or-regexp`.

5.2.3 Global Indexing

Once the index phrases have been collected and organized, you are set for global indexing. I recommend to do this only on an otherwise finished document. Global indexing starts from the phrases buffer. There are several commands which start indexing: *C-c C-x* acts on the current phrase line, *C-c C-r* on all lines in the current region and *C-c C-a* on all phrase lines in the buffer. It is probably good to do indexing in small chunks since your concentration may not last long enough to do everything in one go.

RefTeX will start at the first phrase line and search the phrase globally in the whole document. At each match it will stop, compute the replacement string and offer you the following choices[3]:

y	Replace this match with the proposed string.
n	Skip this match.
!	Replace this and all further matches in this file.
q	Skip this match, start with next file.
Q	Skip this match, start with next phrase.
o	Select a different indexing macro for this match.
1-9	Select one of multiple index keys (those separated with '‖').
e	Edit the replacement text.
C-r	Recursive edit. Use *C-M-c* to return to the indexing process.
s	Save this buffer and ask again about the current match.
S	Save all document buffers and ask again about the current match.
C-g	Abort the indexing process.

The 'Find and Index in Document' menu in the phrases buffer also lists a few options for the indexing process. The options have associated customization variables to set the defaults (see Section 9.6 [Options (Index Support)], page 58). Here is a short explanation of what the options do:

Match Whole Words
> When searching for index phrases, make sure whole words are matched. This should probably always be on.

Case Sensitive Search
> Search case sensitively for phrases. I recommend to have this setting off, in order to match the capitalized words at the beginning of a sentence, and even typos. You can always say *no* at a match you do not like.

Wrap Long Lines
> Inserting index macros increases the line length. Turn this option on to allow RefTeX to wrap long lines.

---

[3] Windows users: Restrict yourself to the described keys during indexing. Pressing HELP at the indexing prompt can apparently hang Emacs.

Skip Indexed Matches

When this is on, RefTEX will at each match try to figure out if this match is already indexed. A match is considered indexed if it is either the argument of an index macro, or if an index macro is directly (without whitespace separation) before or after the match. Index macros are those configured in `reftex-index-macros`. Intended for re-indexing a documents after changes have been made.

Even though indexing should be the last thing you do to a document, you are bound to make changes afterwards. Indexing then has to be applied to the changed regions. The command `reftex-index-phrases-apply-to-region` is designed for this purpose. When called from a LaTeX document with active region, it will apply `reftex-index-all-phrases` to the current region.

5.3 Displaying and Editing the Index

In order to compile and display the index, press `C-c >`. If the document uses multiple indices, RefTEX will ask you to select one. Then, all index entries will be sorted alphabetically and displayed in a special buffer, the '`*Index*`' buffer. From that buffer you can check and edit each entry.

The index can be restricted to the current section or the region. Then only entries in that part of the document will go into the compiled index. To restrict to the current section, use a numeric prefix '2', thus press `C-u 2 C-c >`. To restrict to the current region, make the region active and use a numeric prefix '3' (press `C-u 3 C-c >`). From within the '`*Index*`' buffer the restriction can be moved from one section to the next by pressing the `<` and `>` keys.

One caveat: RefTEX finds the definition point of an index entry by searching near the buffer position where it had found to macro during scanning. If you have several identical index entries in the same buffer and significant changes have shifted the entries around, you must rescan the buffer to ensure the correspondence between the '`*Index*`' buffer and the definition locations. It is therefore advisable to rescan the document (with `r` or `C-u r`) frequently while editing the index from the '`*Index*`' buffer.

Here is a list of special commands available in the '`*Index*`' buffer. A summary of this information is always available by pressing `?`.

General

`?`	Display a summary of commands.
`0-9, -`	Prefix argument.

Moving around

`! A..Z`	Pressing any capital letter will jump to the corresponding section in the '`*Index*`' buffer. The exclamation mark is special and jumps to the first entries alphabetically sorted below '`A`'. These are usually non-alphanumeric characters.
`n`	Go to next entry.
`p`	Go to previous entry.

Access to document locations

SPC	Show the place in the document where this index entry is defined.

TAB   Go to the definition of the current index entry in another window.

RET   Go to the definition of the current index entry and hide the '`*Index*`' buffer window.

f   Toggle follow mode. When follow mode is active, the other window will always show the location corresponding to the line in the '`*Index*`' buffer at point. This is similar to pressing SPC after each cursor motion. The default for this flag can be set with the variable `reftex-index-follow-mode`. Note that only context in files already visited is shown. RefTEX will not visit a file just for follow mode. See, however, the variable `reftex-revisit-to-follow`.

Entry editing

e   Edit the current index entry. In the minibuffer, you can edit the index macro which defines this entry.

C-k   Kill the index entry. Currently not implemented because I don't know how to implement an `undo` function for this.

*   Edit the *key* part of the entry. This is the initial part of the entry which determines the location of the entry in the index.

| Edit the *attribute* part of the entry. This is the part after the vertical bar. With `MakeIndex`, this part is an encapsulating macro. With `xindy`, it is called *attribute* and is a property of the index entry that can lead to special formatting. When called with *C-u* prefix, kill the entire *attribute* part.

@   Edit the *visual* part of the entry. This is the part after the '`@`' which is used by `MakeIndex` to change the visual appearance of the entry in the index. When called with *C-u* prefix, kill the entire *visual* part.

(Toggle the beginning of page range property '`|(`' of the entry.

)   Toggle the end of page range property '`|)`' of the entry.

_   Make the current entry a subentry. This command will prompt for the superordinate entry and insert it.

^   Remove the highest superordinate entry. If the current entry is a subitem ('`aaa!bbb!ccc`'), this function moves it up the hierarchy ('`bbb!ccc`').

Exiting

q   Hide the '`*Index*`' buffer.

k   Kill the '`*Index*`' buffer.

C-c =   Switch to the Table of Contents buffer of this document.

Controlling what gets displayed

c   Toggle the display of short context in the '`*Index*`' buffer. The default for this flag can be set with the variable `reftex-index-include-context`.

}   Restrict the index to a single document section. The corresponding section number will be displayed in the `R<>` indicator in the mode line and in the header of the '`*Index*`' buffer.

{	Widen the index to contain all entries of the document.
<	When the index is currently restricted, move the restriction to the previous section.
>	When the index is currently restricted, move the restriction to the next section.

Updating the buffer

g	Rebuild the '*Index*' buffer. This does *not* rescan the document. However, it sorts the entries again, so that edited entries will move to the correct position.
r	Reparse the LaTeX document and rebuild the '*Index*' buffer. When **reftex-enable-partial-scans** is non-**nil**, rescan only the file this location is defined in, not the entire document.
C-u r	Reparse the *entire* LaTeX document and rebuild the '*Index*' buffer.
s	Switch to a different index (for documents with multiple indices).

5.4 Builtin Index Macros

RefTeX by default recognizes the \index and \glossary macros which are defined in the LaTeX core. It has also builtin support for the re-implementations of \index in the 'multind' and 'index' packages. However, since the different definitions of the \index macro are incompatible, you will have to explicitly specify the index style used. See Section 5.1 [Creating Index Entries], page 24, for information on how to do that.

5.5 Defining Index Macros

When writing a document with an index you will probably define additional macros which make entries into the index. Let's look at an example.

```
\newcommand{\ix}[1]{#1\index{#1}}
\newcommand{\nindex}[1]{\textit{#1}\index[name]{#1}}
\newcommand{\astobj}[1]{\index{Astronomical Objects!#1}}
```

The first macro \ix typesets its argument in the text and places it into the index. The second macro \nindex typesets its argument in the text and places it into a separate index with the tag 'name'[4]. The last macro also places its argument into the index, but as subitems under the main index entry 'Astronomical Objects'. Here is how to make RefTeX recognize and correctly interpret these macros, first with Emacs Lisp.

```
(setq reftex-index-macros
      '(("\\ix{*}" "idx" ?x "" nil nil)
        ("\\nindex{*}" "name" ?n "" nil nil)
        ("\\astobj{*}" "idx" ?o "Astronomical Objects!" nil t)))
```

Note that the index tag is 'idx' for the main index, and 'name' for the name index. 'idx' and 'glo' are reserved for the default index and for the glossary.

The character arguments ?x, ?n, and ?o are for quick identification of these macros when RefTeX inserts new index entries with **reftex-index**. These codes need to be unique. ?i, ?I, and ?g are reserved for the \index, \index*, and \glossary macros, respectively.

---

[4] We are using the syntax of the 'index' package here.

The following string is empty unless your macro adds a superordinate entry to the index key - this is the case for the \astobj macro.

The next entry can be a hook function to exclude certain matches, it almost always can be nil.

The final element in the list indicates if the text being indexed needs to be repeated outside the macro. For the normal index macros, this should be t. Only if the macro typesets the entry in the text (like \ix and \nindex in the example do), this should be nil.

To do the same thing with customize, you need to fill in the templates like this:

```
Repeat:
[INS] [DEL] List:
            Macro with args: \ix{*}
            Index Tag      : [Value Menu] String: idx
            Access Key     : x
            Key Prefix     :
            Exclusion hook : nil
            Repeat Outside : [Toggle]  off (nil)
[INS] [DEL] List:
            Macro with args: \nindex{*}
            Index Tag      : [Value Menu] String: name
            Access Key     : n
            Key Prefix     :
            Exclusion hook : nil
            Repeat Outside : [Toggle]  off (nil)
[INS] [DEL] List:
            Macro with args: \astobj{*}
            Index Tag      : [Value Menu] String: idx
            Access Key     : o
            Key Prefix     : Astronomical Objects!
            Exclusion hook : nil
            Repeat Outside : [Toggle]  on (non-nil)
[INS]
```

With the macro \ix defined, you may want to change the default macro used for indexing a text phrase (see Section 5.1 [Creating Index Entries], page 24). This would be done like this

```
(setq reftex-index-default-macro '(?x "idx"))
```

which specifies that the macro identified with the character ?x (the \ix macro) should be used for indexing phrases and words already in the buffer with *C-c /* (reftex-index-selection-or-word). The index tag is "idx".

6 Viewing Cross-References

RefTEX can display cross-referencing information. This means, if two document locations are linked, RefTEX can display the matching location(s) in another window. The \label and \ref macros are one way of establishing such a link. Also, a \cite macro is linked to the corresponding \bibitem macro or a BibTEX database entry.

The feature is invoked by pressing *C-c &* (reftex-view-crossref) while point is on the *key* argument of a macro involved in cross-referencing. You can also click with *S-mouse-2* on the macro argument. Here is what will happen for individual classes of macros:

\ref   Display the corresponding label definition. All usual variants[1] of the \ref macro are active for cross-reference display. This works also for labels defined in an external document when the current document refers to them through the xr interface (see Section 3.7 [xr (LaTeX package)], page 19).

\label   Display a document location which references this label. Pressing *C-c &* several times moves through the entire document and finds all locations. Not only the \label macro but also other macros with label arguments (as configured with reftex-label-alist) are active for cross-reference display.

\cite   Display the corresponding BibTEX database entry or \bibitem. All usual variants[2] of the \cite macro are active for cross-reference display.

\bibitem   Display a document location which cites this article. Pressing *C-c &* several times moves through the entire document and finds all locations.

BibTEX   *C-c &* is also active in BibTEX buffers. All locations in a document where the database entry at point is cited will be displayed. On first use, RefTEX will prompt for a buffer which belongs to the document you want to search. Subsequent calls will use the same document, until you break this link with a prefix argument to *C-c &*.

\index   Display other locations in the document which are marked by an index macro with the same key argument. Along with the standard \index and \glossary macros, all macros configured in reftex-index-macros will be recognized.

While the display of cross referencing information for the above mentioned macros is hard-coded, you can configure additional relations in the variable reftex-view-crossref-extra.

---

[1] all macros that start with 'ref' or end with 'ref' or 'refrange'

[2] all macros that either start or end with 'cite'

7 All the Rest

7.1 RefTEX's Menu

RefTEX installs a `Ref` menu in the menu bar on systems which support this. From this menu you can access all of RefTEX's commands and a few of its options. There is also a `Customize` submenu which can be used to access RefTEX's entire set of options.

7.2 Default Key Bindings

Here is a summary of the available key bindings.

```
C-c =      reftex-toc
C-c -      reftex-toc-recenter
C-c (      reftex-label
C-c )      reftex-reference
C-c [      reftex-citation
C-c &      reftex-view-crossref
S-mouse-2  reftex-mouse-view-crossref
C-c /      reftex-index-selection-or-word
C-c \      reftex-index-phrase-selection-or-word
C-c |      reftex-index-visit-phrases-buffer
C-c <      reftex-index
C-c >      reftex-display-index
```

Note that the *S-mouse-2* binding is only provided if this key is not already used by some other package. RefTEX will not override an existing binding to *S-mouse-2*.

Personally, I also bind some functions in the users *C-c* map for easier access.

```
C-c t      reftex-toc
C-c l      reftex-label
C-c r      reftex-reference
C-c c      reftex-citation
C-c v      reftex-view-crossref
C-c s      reftex-search-document
C-c g      reftex-grep-document
```

These keys are reserved for the user, so I cannot bind them by default. If you want to have these key bindings available, set in your '.emacs' file:

```
(setq reftex-extra-bindings t)
```

Changing and adding to RefTEX's key bindings is best done in the hook `reftex-load-hook`. For information on the keymaps which should be used to add keys, see Section 9.12 [Keymaps and Hooks], page 67.

7.3 Faces

RefTEX uses faces when available to structure the selection and table of contents buffers. It does not create its own faces, but uses the ones defined in 'font-lock.el'. Therefore, RefTEX will use faces only when `font-lock` is loaded. This seems to be reasonable because people who like faces will very likely have it loaded. If you wish to turn off fontification or change the involved faces, see Section 9.10 [Options (Fontification)], page 65.

7.4 Multifile Documents

The following is relevant when working with documents spread over many files:

- RefTEX has full support for multifile documents. You can edit parts of several (multi-file) documents at the same time without conflicts. RefTEX provides functions to run `grep`, `search` and `query-replace` on all files which are part of a multifile document.

- All files belonging to a multifile document should define a File Variable (`TeX-master` for AUCTEX or `tex-main-file` for the standard Emacs LATEX mode) containing the name of the master file. For example, to set the file variable `TeX-master`, include something like the following at the end of each TEX file:

      %%% Local Variables: ***
      %%% mode:latex ***
      %%% TeX-master: "thesis.tex" ***
      %%% End: ***

  AUCTEX with the setting

      (setq-default TeX-master nil)

  will actually ask you for each new file about the master file and insert this comment automatically. For more details see the documentation of the AUCTEX (see Section "Multifile" in *The AUCTeX User Manual*), the documentation about the Emacs (La)TeX mode (see Section "TeX Print" in *The GNU Emacs Manual*) and the Emacs documentation on File Variables (see Section "File Variables" in *The GNU Emacs Manual*).

- The context of a label definition must be found in the same file as the label itself in order to be processed correctly by RefTEX. The only exception is that section labels referring to a section statement outside the current file can still use that section title as context.

7.5 Language Support

Some parts of RefTEX are language dependent. The default settings work well for English. If you are writing in a different language, the following hints may be useful:

- The mechanism to derive a label from context includes the abbreviation of words and omission of unimportant words. These mechanisms may have to be changed for other languages. See the variables `reftex-derive-label-parameters` and `reftex-abbrev-parameters`.

- Also, when a label is derived from context, RefTEX clears the context string from non-ASCII characters in order to make a valid label. If there should ever be a version of TEX which allows extended characters *in labels*, then we will have to look at the variables `reftex-translate-to-ascii-function` and `reftex-label-illegal-re`.

- When a label is referenced, RefTEX looks at the word before point to guess which label type is required. These *magic words* are different in every language. For an example of how to add magic words, see Section 3.4.4 [Adding Magic Words], page 15.

- RefTEX inserts "punctuation" for multiple references and for the author list in citations. Some of this may be language dependent. See the variables `reftex-multiref-punctuation` and `reftex-cite-punctuation`.

7.6 Finding Files

In order to find files included in a document via \input or \include, RefTeX searches all directories specified in the environment variable TEXINPUTS. Similarly, it will search the path specified in the variables BIBINPUTS and TEXBIB for BibTeX database files.

When searching, RefTeX will also expand recursive path definitions (directories ending in '//' or '!!'). But it will only search and expand directories *explicitly* given in these variables. This may cause problems under the following circumstances:

- Most TeX system have a default search path for both TeX files and BibTeX files which is defined in some setup file. Usually this default path is for system files which RefTeX does not need to see. But if your document needs TeX files or BibTeX database files in a directory only given in the default search path, RefTeX will fail to find them.

- Some TeX systems do not use environment variables at all in order to specify the search path. Both default and user search path are then defined in setup files.

There are three ways to solve this problem:

- Specify all relevant directories explicitly in the environment variables. If for some reason you don't want to mess with the default variables TEXINPUTS and BIBINPUTS, define your own variables and configure RefTeX to use them instead:

```
(setq reftex-texpath-environment-variables '("MYTEXINPUTS"))
(setq reftex-bibpath-environment-variables '("MYBIBINPUTS"))
```

- Specify the full search path directly in RefTeX's variables.

```
(setq reftex-texpath-environment-variables
      '("./inp:/home/cd/tex//:/usr/local/tex//"))
(setq reftex-bibpath-environment-variables
      '("/home/cd/tex/lit/"))
```

- Some TeX systems provide stand-alone programs to do the file search just like TeX and BibTeX. E.g. Thomas Esser's teTeX uses the kpathsearch library which provides the command kpsewhich to search for files. RefTeX can be configured to use this program. Note that the exact syntax of the kpsewhich command depends upon the version of that program.

```
(setq reftex-use-external-file-finders t)
(setq reftex-external-file-finders
      '(("tex" . "kpsewhich -format=.tex %f")
        ("bib" . "kpsewhich -format=.bib %f")))
```

Some people like to use RefTeX with noweb files, which usually have the extension '.nw'. In order to deal with such files, the new extension must be added to the list of valid extensions in the variable reftex-file-extensions. When working with AUCTeX as major mode, the new extension must also be known to AUCTeX via the variable TeX-file-extension. For example:

```
(setq reftex-file-extensions
      '(("nw" "tex" ".tex" ".ltx") ("bib" ".bib")))
(setq TeX-file-extensions
      '( "nw" "tex" "sty" "cls" "ltx" "texi" "texinfo"))
```

7.7 Optimizations

Note added 2002. Computers have gotten a lot faster, so most of the optimizations discussed below will not be necessary on new machines. I am leaving this stuff in the manual for people who want to write thick books, where some of it still might be useful.

Implementing the principle of least surprises, the default settings of RefTeX ensure a safe ride for beginners and casual users. However, when using RefTeX for a large project and/or on a small computer, there are ways to improve speed or memory usage.

- **Removing Lookup Buffers**
  RefTeX will load other parts of a multifile document as well as BibTeX database files for lookup purposes. These buffers are kept, so that subsequent use of the same files is fast. If you can't afford keeping these buffers around, and if you can live with a speed penalty, try

  ```
  (setq reftex-keep-temporary-buffers nil)
  ```

- **Partial Document Scans**
  A `C-u` prefix on the major RefTeX commands `reftex-label` (`C-u C-c ()`, `reftex-reference` (`C-u C-c )`), `reftex-citation` (`C-u C-c [`), `reftex-toc` (`C-u C-c =`), and `reftex-view-crossref` (`C-u C-c &`) initiates re-parsing of the entire document in order to update the parsing information. For a large document this can be unnecessary, in particular if only one file has changed. RefTeX can be configured to do partial scans instead of full ones. `C-u` re-parsing then does apply only to the current buffer and files included from it. Likewise, the `r` key in both the label selection buffer and the table-of-contents buffer will only prompt scanning of the file in which the label or section macro near the cursor was defined. Re-parsing of the entire document is still available by using `C-u C-u` as a prefix, or the capital `R` key in the menus. To use this feature, try

  ```
  (setq reftex-enable-partial-scans t)
  ```

- **Saving Parser Information**
  Even with partial scans enabled, RefTeX still has to make one full scan, when you start working with a document. To avoid this, parsing information can be stored in a file. The file 'MASTER.rel' is used for storing information about a document with master file 'MASTER.tex'. It is written automatically when you kill a buffer in **reftex-mode** or when you exit Emacs. The information is restored when you begin working with a document in a new editing session. To use this feature, put into '.emacs':

  ```
  (setq reftex-save-parse-info t)
  ```

- **Identifying label types by prefix**
  RefTeX normally parses around each label to check in which environment this label is located, in order to assign a label type to the label. If your document contains thousands of labels, document parsing will take considerable time. If you have been using label prefixes like tab: and fn: consistently, you can tell RefTeX to get the label type directly from the prefix, without additional parsing. This will be faster and also allow labels to end up in the correct category if for some reason it is not possible to derive the correct type from context. For example, to enable this feature for footnote and equation labels, use

  ```
  (setq reftex-trust-label-prefix '("fn:" "eq:"))
  ```

- **Automatic Document Scans**

  At rare occasions, RefTEX will automatically rescan a part of the document. If this gets into your way, it can be turned off with

  ```
  (setq reftex-allow-automatic-rescan nil)
  ```

  RefTEX will then occasionally annotate new labels in the selection buffer, saying that their position in the label list in uncertain. A manual document scan will fix this.

- **Multiple Selection Buffers**

  Normally, the selection buffer '*RefTeX Select*' is re-created for every selection process. In documents with very many labels this can take several seconds. RefTEX provides an option to create a separate selection buffer for each label type and to keep this buffer from one selection to the next. These buffers are updated automatically only when a new label has been added in the buffers category with `reftex-label`. Updating the buffer takes as long as recreating it - so the time saving is limited to cases where no new labels of that category have been added. To turn on this feature, use

  ```
  (setq reftex-use-multiple-selection-buffers t)
  ```

  You can also inhibit the automatic updating entirely. Then the selection buffer will always pop up very fast, but may not contain the most recently defined labels. You can always update the buffer by hand, with the *g* key. To get this behavior, use instead

  ```
  (setq reftex-use-multiple-selection-buffers t
        reftex-auto-update-selection-buffers nil)
  ```

As a summary, here are the settings I recommend for heavy use of RefTEX with large documents:

```
(setq reftex-enable-partial-scans t
      reftex-save-parse-info t
      reftex-use-multiple-selection-buffers t)
```

7.8 AUCTEX

AUCTEX is without doubt the best major mode for editing TEX and LATEX files with Emacs (see Section "Top" in *The AUCTeX User Manual*). If AUCTEX is not part of your Emacs distribution, you can get it[1] by FTP from the AUCTEX web site.

7.8.1 The AUCTEX-RefTEX Interface

RefTEX contains code to interface with AUCTEX. When this interface is turned on, both packages will interact closely. Instead of using RefTEX's commands directly, you can then also use them indirectly as part of the AUCTEX environment[2]. The interface is turned on with

```
(setq reftex-plug-into-AUCTeX t)
```

If you need finer control about which parts of the interface are used and which not, read the docstring of the variable `reftex-plug-into-AUCTeX` or customize it with *M-x customize-variable RET reftex-plug-into-AUCTeX RET*.

---

[1] XEmacs 21.x users may want to install the corresponding XEmacs package.

[2] RefTEX 4.0 and AUCTEX 9.10c will be needed for all of this to work. Parts of it work also with earlier versions.

The following list describes the individual parts of the interface.

- **AUCTₑX calls `reftex-label` to insert labels**
  When a new section is created with *C-c C-s*, or a new environment is inserted with *C-c C-e*, AUCTₑX normally prompts for a label to go with it. With the interface, `reftex-label` is called instead. For example, if you type *C-c C-e equation RET*, AUCTₑX and RefTₑX will insert

      \begin{equation}
      \label{eq:1}

      \end{equation}

  without further prompts.

  Similarly, when you type *C-c C-s section RET*, RefTₑX will offer its default label which is derived from the section title.

- **AUCTₑX tells RefTₑX about new sections**
  When creating a new section with *C-c C-s*, RefTₑX will not have to rescan the buffer in order to see it.

- **RefTₑX supplies macro arguments**
  When you insert a macro interactively with *C-c RET*, AUCTₑX normally prompts for macro arguments. Internally, it uses the functions `TeX-arg-label`, `TeX-arg-cite`, and `TeX-arg-index` to prompt for arguments which are labels, citation keys and index entries. The interface takes over these functions[3] and supplies the macro arguments with **RefTₑX**'s mechanisms. For example, when you type *C-c RET ref RET*, RefTₑX will supply its label selection process (see Section 3.2 [Referencing Labels], page 9).

- **RefTₑX tells AUCTₑX about new labels, citation and index keys**
  RefTₑX will add all newly created labels to AUCTₑX's completion list.

7.8.2 Style Files

Style files are Emacs Lisp files which are evaluated by AUCTₑX in association with the `\documentclass` and `\usepackage` commands of a document (see Section 7.8.2 [Style Files], page 38). Support for RefTₑX in such a style file is useful when the LATₑX style defines macros or environments connected with labels, citations, or the index. Many style files (e.g. 'amsmath.el' or 'natbib.el') distributed with AUCTₑX already support RefTₑX in this way.

Before calling a RefTₑX function, the style hook should always test for the availability of the function, so that the style file will also work for people who do not use RefTₑX.

Additions made with style files in the way described below remain local to the current document. For example, if one package uses AMSTeX, the style file will make RefTₑX switch over to `\eqref`, but this will not affect other documents.

A style hook may contain calls to **`reftex-add-label-environments`**[4] which defines additions to `reftex-label-alist`. The argument taken by this function must have the

---

[3] `fset` is used to do this, which is not reversible. However, RefTₑX implements the old functionality when you later decide to turn off the interface.

[4] This used to be the function `reftex-add-to-label-alist` which is still available as an alias for compatibility.

same format as `reftex-label-alist`. The '`amsmath.el`' style file of AUCTEX for example contains the following:

```
(TeX-add-style-hook "amsmath"
    (lambda ()
      (if (fboundp 'reftex-add-label-environments)
          (reftex-add-label-environments '(AMSTeX)))))
```

while a package `myprop` defining a `proposition` environment with `\newtheorem` might use

```
(TeX-add-style-hook "myprop"
    (lambda ()
      (LaTeX-add-environments '("proposition" LaTeX-env-label))
      (if (fboundp 'reftex-add-label-environments)
          (reftex-add-label-environments
           '(("proposition" ?p "prop:" "~\\ref{%s}" t
                            ("Proposition" "Prop.") -3))))))
```

Similarly, a style hook may contain a call to `reftex-set-cite-format` to set the citation format. The style file '`natbib.el`' for the Natbib citation style does switch RefTEX's citation format like this:

```
(TeX-add-style-hook "natbib"
    (lambda ()
      (if (fboundp 'reftex-set-cite-format)
          (reftex-set-cite-format 'natbib))))
```

The hook may contain a call to `reftex-add-index-macros` to define additional `\index`-like macros. The argument must have the same format as `reftex-index-macros`. It may be a symbol, to trigger support for one of the builtin index packages. For example, the style '`multind.el`' contains

```
(TeX-add-style-hook "multind"
  (lambda ()
    (and (fboundp 'reftex-add-index-macros)
(reftex-add-index-macros '(multind)))))
```

If you have your own package '`myindex`' which defines the following macros to be used with the LaTeX '`index.sty`' file

```
\newcommand{\molec}[1]{#1\index{Molecules!#1}}
\newcommand{\aindex}[1]{#1\index[author]{#1}
```

you could write this in the style file '`myindex.el`':

```
(TeX-add-style-hook "myindex"
    (lambda ()
      (TeX-add-symbols
       '("molec" TeX-arg-index)
       '("aindex" TeX-arg-index))
      (if (fboundp 'reftex-add-index-macros)
          (reftex-add-index-macros
           '(("molec{*}" "idx" ?m "Molecules!" nil nil)
             ("aindex{*}" "author" ?a "" nil nil))))))
```

Finally the hook may contain a call to `reftex-add-section-levels` to define additional section statements. For example, the FoilTeX class has just two headers, `\foilhead` and `\rotatefoilhead`. Here is a style file 'foils.el' that will inform RefTeX about these:

```
(TeX-add-style-hook "foils"
   (lambda ()
      (if (fboundp 'reftex-add-section-levels)
          (reftex-add-section-levels '(("foilhead" . 3)
                                       ("rotatefoilhead" . 3)))))))
```

7.8.3 Bib-Cite

Once you have written a document with labels, references and citations, it can be nice to read it like a hypertext document. RefTeX has support for that: `reftex-view-crossref` (bound to *C-c &*), `reftex-mouse-view-crossref` (bound to *S-mouse-2*), and `reftex-search-document`. A somewhat fancier interface with mouse highlighting is provided (among other things) by Peter S. Galbraith's 'bib-cite.el'. There is some overlap in the functionalities of Bib-cite and RefTeX. Bib-cite.el comes bundled with AUCTeX.

Bib-cite version 3.06 and later can be configured so that bib-cite's mouse functions use RefTeX for displaying references and citations. This can be useful in particular when working with the LaTeX `xr` package or with an explicit `thebibliography` environment (rather than BibTeX). Bib-cite cannot handle those, but RefTeX does. To make use of this feature, try

```
(setq bib-cite-use-reftex-view-crossref t)
```

7.9 Problems and Work-arounds

- **LaTeX commands**
  \input, \include, and \section (etc.) statements have to be first on a line (except for white space).

- **Commented regions**
  RefTEX sees also labels in regions commented out and will refuse to make duplicates of such labels. This is considered to be a feature.

- **Wrong section numbers**
  When using partial scans (`reftex-enable-partial-scans`), the section numbers in the table of contents may eventually become wrong. A full scan will fix this.

- **Local settings**
  The label environment definitions in `reftex-label-alist` are global and apply to all documents. If you need to make definitions local to a document, because they would interfere with settings in other documents, you should use AUCTEX and set up style files with calls to `reftex-add-label-environments`, `reftex-set-cite-format`, `reftex-add-index-macros`, and `reftex-add-section-levels`. Settings made with these functions remain local to the current document. See Section 7.8 [AUCTeX], page 37.

- **Funny display in selection buffer**
  When using packages which make the buffer representation of a file different from its disk representation (e.g. x-symbol, isotex, iso-cvt) you may find that RefTEX's parsing information sometimes reflects the disk state of a file. This happens only in *unvisited* parts of a multifile document, because RefTEX visits these files literally for speed reasons. Then both short context and section headings may look different from what you usually see on your screen. In rare cases `reftex-toc` may have problems to jump to an affected section heading. There are three possible ways to deal with this:

  - (setq reftex-keep-temporary-buffers t)
    This implies that RefTEX will load all parts of a multifile document into Emacs (i.e. there won't be any temporary buffers).

  - (setq reftex-initialize-temporary-buffers t)
    This means full initialization of temporary buffers. It involves a penalty when the same unvisited file is used for lookup often.

  - Set `reftex-initialize-temporary-buffers` to a list of hook functions doing a minimal initialization.

  See also the variable `reftex-refontify-context`.

- **Labels as arguments to \begin**
  Some packages use an additional argument to a \begin macro to specify a label. E.g. Lamport's 'pf.sty' uses both

  > \step{*label*}{*claim*}   and   \begin{step+}{*label*}
  >   *claim*
  >   \end{step+}

  We need to trick RefTEX into swallowing this:

```
;; Configuration for Lamport's pf.sty
(setq reftex-label-alist
  '(("\\step{*}{}"        ?p "st:" "~\\stepref{%s}" 2 ("Step" "St."))
    ("\\begin{step+}{*}" ?p "st:" "~\\stepref{%s}" 1000)))
```

The first line is just a normal configuration for a macro. For the **step+** environment we actually tell RefTEX to look for the *macro* '\begin{step+}' and interpret the *first* argument (which really is a second argument to the macro \begin) as a label of type **?p**. Argument count for this macro starts only after the '{step+}', also when specifying how to get context.

- **Idle timers in XEmacs**
  In XEmacs, idle timer restart does not work reliably after fast keystrokes. Therefore RefTEX currently uses the post command hook to start the timer used for automatic crossref information. When this bug gets fixed, a real idle timer can be requested with

  ```
  (setq reftex-use-itimer-in-xemacs t)
  ```

- **Viper mode**
  With *Viper* mode prior to Vipers version 3.01, you need to protect RefTEX's keymaps with

  ```
  (viper-harness-minor-mode "reftex")
  ```

7.10 Imprint

RefTEX was written by *Carsten Dominik* dominik@science.uva.nl, with contributions by *Stephen Eglen*. RefTEX is currently maintained by the AUCTEX project, see the AUCTEX web site for detailed information.

If you have questions about RefTEX, you can send email to the AUCTEX user mailing list (auctex@gnu.org). If you want to contribute code or ideas, write to the AUCTEX developer mailing list (auctex-devel@gnu.org). And in the rare case of finding a bug, please use *M-x reftex-report-bug RET* which will prepare a bug report with useful information about your setup. Remember to add essential information like a recipe for reproducing the bug, what you expected to happen, and what actually happened. Send the bug report to the AUCTEX bug mailing list (bug-auctex@gnu.org).

There are also several Usenet groups which have competent readers who might be able to help: comp.emacs, gnu.emacs.help, comp.emacs.xemacs, and comp.text.tex.

Thanks to the people on the Net who have used RefTEX and helped developing it with their reports. In particular thanks to *Ralf Angeli, Fran Burstall, Alastair Burt, Lars Clausen, Soren Dayton, Stephen Eglen, Karl Eichwalder, Erik Frisk, Peter Galbraith, Kai Grossjohann, Frank Harrell, Till A. Heilmann, Peter Heslin, Stephan Heuel, Alan Ho, Lute Kamstra, Dieter Kraft, David Kastrup, Adrian Lanz, Juri Linkov, Wolfgang Mayer, Rory Molinari, Stefan Monnier, Laurent Mugnier, Dan Nicolaescu, Sudeep Kumar Palat, Daniel Polani, Alan Shutko, Robin Socha, Richard Stanton, Allan Strand, Jan Vroonhof, Christoph Wedler, Alan Williams, Roland Winkler, Hans-Christoph Wirth, Eli Zaretskii.*

The view-crossref feature was inspired by *Peter Galbraith's* 'bib-cite.el'.

Finally thanks to *Uwe Bolick* who first got me interested in supporting LATEX labels and references with an editor (which was MicroEmacs at the time).

8 Commands

Here is a summary of RefTEX's commands which can be executed from LATEX files. Command which are executed from the special buffers are not described here. All commands are available from the **Ref** menu. See See Section 7.2 [Key Bindings], page 33.

reftex-toc   [Command]

> Show the table of contents for the current document. When called with one ore two *C-u* prefixes, rescan the document first.

reftex-label   [Command]

> Insert a unique label. With one or two *C-u* prefixes, enforce document rescan first.

reftex-reference   [Command]

> Start a selection process to select a label, and insert a reference to it. With one or two *C-u* prefixes, enforce document rescan first.

reftex-citation   [Command]

> Make a citation using BibTEX database files. After prompting for a regular expression, scans the buffers with BibTEX entries (taken from the \bibliography command or a thebibliography environment) and offers the matching entries for selection. The selected entry is formatted according to **reftex-cite-format** and inserted into the buffer.
>
> When called with a *C-u* prefix, prompt for optional arguments in cite macros. When called with a numeric prefix, make that many citations. When called with point inside the braces of a \cite command, it will add another key, ignoring the value of **reftex-cite-format**.
>
> The regular expression uses an expanded syntax: '&&' is interpreted as **and**. Thus, 'aaaa&&bbb' matches entries which contain both 'aaaa' and 'bbb'. While entering the regexp, completion on knows citation keys is possible. '=' is a good regular expression to match all entries in all files.

reftex-index   [Command]

> Query for an index macro and insert it along with its arguments. The index macros available are those defined in **reftex-index-macro** or by a call to **reftex-add-index-macros**, typically from an AUCTEX style file. RefTEX provides completion for the index tag and the index key, and will prompt for other arguments.

reftex-index-selection-or-word   [Command]

> Put current selection or the word near point into the default index macro. This uses the information in **reftex-index-default-macro** to make an index entry. The phrase indexed is the current selection or the word near point. When called with one *C-u* prefix, let the user have a chance to edit the index entry. When called with 2 *C-u* as prefix, also ask for the index macro and other stuff. When called inside TEX math mode as determined by the 'texmathp.el' library which is part of AUCTEX, the string is first processed with the **reftex-index-math-format**, which see.

reftex-index-phrase-selection-or-word   [Command]

> Add current selection or the word at point to the phrases buffer. When you are in transient-mark-mode and the region is active, the selection will be used - otherwise

the word at point. You get a chance to edit the entry in the phrases buffer - to save the buffer and return to the LATEX document, finish with *C-c C-c*.

reftex-index-visit-phrases-buffer   [Command]
Switch to the phrases buffer, initialize if empty.

reftex-index-phrases-apply-to-region   [Command]
Index all index phrases in the current region. This works exactly like global indexing from the index phrases buffer, but operation is restricted to the current region.

reftex-display-index   [Command]
Display a buffer with an index compiled from the current document. When the document has multiple indices, first prompts for the correct one. When index support is turned off, offer to turn it on. With one or two *C-u* prefixes, rescan document first. With prefix 2, restrict index to current document section. With prefix 3, restrict index to active region.

reftex-view-crossref   [Command]
View cross reference of macro at point. Point must be on the *key* argument. Works with the macros `\label`, `\ref`, `\cite`, `\bibitem`, `\index` and many derivatives of these. Where it makes sense, subsequent calls show additional locations. See also the variable `reftex-view-crossref-extra` and the command `reftex-view-crossref-from-bibtex`. With one or two *C-u* prefixes, enforce rescanning of the document. With argument 2, select the window showing the cross reference.

reftex-view-crossref-from-bibtex   [Command]
View location in a LATEX document which cites the BibTEX entry at point. Since BibTEX files can be used by many LATEX documents, this function prompts upon first use for a buffer in RefTEX mode. To reset this link to a document, call the function with a prefix arg. Calling this function several times find successive citation locations.

reftex-create-tags-file   [Command]
Create TAGS file by running `etags` on the current document. The TAGS file is also immediately visited with `visit-tags-table`.

reftex-grep-document   [Command]
Run grep query through all files related to this document. With prefix arg, force to rescan document. No active TAGS table is required.

reftex-search-document   [Command]
Regexp search through all files of the current document. Starts always in the master file. Stops when a match is found. No active TAGS table is required.

reftex-query-replace-document   [Command]
Run a query-replace-regexp of *from* with *to* over the entire document. With prefix arg, replace only word-delimited matches. No active TAGS table is required.

reftex-isearch-minor-mode   [Command]
Toggle a minor mode which enables incremental search to work globally on the entire multifile document. Files will be searched in the sequence they appear in the document.

`reftex-goto-label`   [Command]

Prompt for a label (with completion) and jump to the location of this label. Optional prefix argument *other-window* goes to the label in another window.

`reftex-change-label`   [Command]

Query replace *from* with *to* in all `\label` and `\ref` commands. Works on the entire multifile document. No active TAGS table is required.

`reftex-renumber-simple-labels`   [Command]

Renumber all simple labels in the document to make them sequentially. Simple labels are the ones created by RefTeX, consisting only of the prefix and a number. After the command completes, all these labels will have sequential numbers throughout the document. Any references to the labels will be changed as well. For this, RefTeX looks at the arguments of any macros which either start or end with the string 'ref'. This command should be used with care, in particular in multifile documents. You should not use it if another document refers to this one with the `xr` package.

`reftex-find-duplicate-labels`   [Command]

Produce a list of all duplicate labels in the document.

`reftex-create-bibtex-file`   [Command]

Create a new BibTeX database file with all entries referenced in document. The command prompts for a filename and writes the collected entries to that file. Only entries referenced in the current document with any `\cite`-like macros are used. The sequence in the new file is the same as it was in the old database.

Entries referenced from other entries must appear after all referencing entries.

You can define strings to be used as header or footer for the created files in the variables `reftex-create-bibtex-header` or `reftex-create-bibtex-footer` respectively.

`reftex-customize`   [Command]

Run the customize browser on the RefTeX group.

`reftex-show-commentary`   [Command]

Show the commentary section from '`reftex.el`'.

`reftex-info`   [Command]

Run info on the top RefTeX node.

`reftex-parse-document`   [Command]

Parse the entire document in order to update the parsing information.

`reftex-reset-mode`   [Command]

Enforce rebuilding of several internal lists and variables. Also removes the parse file associated with the current document.

9 Options, Keymaps, Hooks

Here is a complete list of RefTeX's configuration variables. All variables have customize support - so if you are not familiar with Emacs Lisp (and even if you are) you might find it more comfortable to use `customize` to look at and change these variables. *M-x reftex-customize* will get you there.

9.1 Table of Contents

`reftex-include-file-commands`   [User Option]

> List of LaTeX commands which input another file. The file name is expected after the command, either in braces or separated by whitespace.

`reftex-max-section-depth`   [User Option]

> Maximum depth of section levels in document structure. Standard LaTeX needs 7, default is 12.

`reftex-section-levels`   [User Option]

> Commands and levels used for defining sections in the document. The `car` of each cons cell is the name of the section macro. The `cdr` is a number indicating its level. A negative level means the same as the positive value, but the section will never get a number. The `cdr` may also be a function which then has to return the level. This list is also used for promotion and demotion of sectioning commands. If you are using a document class which has several sets of sectioning commands, promotion only works correctly if this list is sorted first by set, then within each set by level. The promotion commands always select the nearest entry with the correct new level.

`reftex-toc-max-level`   [User Option]

> The maximum level of toc entries which will be included in the TOC. Section headings with a bigger level will be ignored. In RefTeX, chapters are level 1, sections level 2 etc. This variable can be changed from within the '*toc*' buffer with the t key.

`reftex-part-resets-chapter`   [User Option]

> Non-`nil` means, \part is like any other sectioning command. This means, part numbers will be included in the numbering of chapters, and chapter counters will be reset for each part. When `nil` (the default), parts are special, do not reset the chapter counter and also do not show up in chapter numbers.

`reftex-auto-recenter-toc`   [User Option]

> Non-`nil` means, turn automatic recentering of '*TOC*' window on. When active, the '*TOC*' window will always show the section you are currently working in. Recentering happens whenever Emacs is idle for more than `reftex-idle-time` seconds.

> Value `t` means, turn on immediately when RefTeX gets started. Then, recentering will work for any toc window created during the session.

> Value `frame` (the default) means, turn automatic recentering on only while the dedicated TOC frame does exist, and do the recentering only in that frame. So when creating that frame (with d key in an ordinary TOC window), the automatic recentering is turned on. When the frame gets destroyed, automatic recentering is turned off again.

This feature can be turned on and off from the menu (Ref->Options).

`reftex-toc-split-windows-horizontally`   [User Option]
> Non-`nil` means, create TOC window by splitting window horizontally. The default is to split vertically.

`reftex-toc-split-windows-fraction`   [User Option]
> Fraction of the width or height of the frame to be used for TOC window.

`reftex-toc-keep-other-windows`   [User Option]
> Non-`nil` means, split the selected window to display the '`*toc*`' buffer. This helps to keep the window configuration, but makes the '`*toc*`' small. When `nil`, all other windows except the selected one will be deleted, so that the '`*toc*`' window fills half the frame.

`reftex-toc-include-file-boundaries`   [User Option]
> Non-`nil` means, include file boundaries in '`*toc*`' buffer. This flag can be toggled from within the '`*toc*`' buffer with the *i* key.

`reftex-toc-include-labels`   [User Option]
> Non-`nil` means, include labels in '`*toc*`' buffer. This flag can be toggled from within the '`*toc*`' buffer with the *l* key.

`reftex-toc-include-index-entries`   [User Option]
> Non-`nil` means, include index entries in '`*toc*`' buffer. This flag can be toggled from within the '`*toc*`' buffer with the *i* key.

`reftex-toc-include-context`   [User Option]
> Non-`nil` means, include context with labels in the '`*toc*`' buffer. Context will only be shown if the labels are visible as well. This flag can be toggled from within the '`*toc*`' buffer with the *c* key.

`reftex-toc-follow-mode`   [User Option]
> Non-`nil` means, point in '`*toc*`' buffer (the table-of-contents buffer) will cause other window to follow. The other window will show the corresponding part of the document. This flag can be toggled from within the '`*toc*`' buffer with the *f* key.

`reftex-toc-mode-hook`   [Normal Hook]
> Normal hook which is run when a '`*toc*`' buffer is created.

`reftex-toc-map`   [Keymap]
> The keymap which is active in the '`*toc*`' buffer. (see Chapter 2 [Table of Contents], page 5).

9.2 Defining Label Environments

`reftex-default-label-alist-entries`   [User Option]
> Default label alist specifications. It is a list of symbols with associations in the constant `reftex-label-alist-builtin`. LaTeX should always be the last entry.

`reftex-label-alist`   [User Option]

> Set this variable to define additions and changes to the defaults in `reftex-default-label-alist-entries`. The only things you *must not* change is that `?s` is the type indicator for section labels, and SPC for the `any` label type. These are hard-coded at other places in the code.
>
> The value of the variable must be a list of items. Each item is a list itself and has the following structure:
>
> > (*env-or-macro type-key label-prefix reference-format*
> > *context-method (magic-word ...) toc-level*)
>
> Each list entry describes either an environment carrying a counter for use with `\label` and `\ref`, or a LaTeX macro defining a label as (or inside) one of its arguments. The elements of each list entry are:

env-or-macro

> Name of the environment (like '`table`') or macro (like '`\myfig`'). For macros, indicate the arguments, as in '`\myfig[]{}{}{*}{}`'. Use square brackets for optional arguments, a star to mark the label argument, if any. The macro does not have to have a label argument - you could also use '`\label{...}`' inside one of its arguments.
>
> Special names: `section` for section labels, `any` to define a group which contains all labels.
>
> This may also be a function to do local parsing and identify point to be in a non-standard label environment. The function must take an argument *bound* and limit backward searches to this value. It should return either nil or a cons cell (*function . position*) with the function symbol and the position where the special environment starts. See the Info documentation for an example.
>
> Finally this may also be `nil` if the entry is only meant to change some settings associated with the type indicator character (see below).

type-key Type indicator character, like `?t`, must be a printable ASCII character. The type indicator is a single character which defines a label type. Any label inside the environment or macro is assumed to belong to this type. The same character may occur several times in this list, to cover cases in which different environments carry the same label type (like `equation` and `eqnarray`). If the type indicator is `nil` and the macro has a label argument '`{*}`', the macro defines neutral labels just like `\label`. In this case the remainder of this entry is ignored.

label-prefix

> Label prefix string, like '`tab:`'. The prefix is a short string used as the start of a label. It may be the empty string. The prefix may contain the following '`%`' escapes:
>
> > `%f` Current file name, directory and extension stripped.
> > `%F` Current file name relative to master file directory.
> > `%m` Master file name, directory and extension stripped.
> > `%M` Directory name (without path) where master file is located.

```
%u User login name, on systems which support this.
%S A section prefix derived with variable reftex-section-
prefixes.
```

Example: In a file 'intro.tex', 'eq:%f:' will become 'eq:intro:'.

reference-format

Format string for reference insertion in buffer. '%s' will be replaced by the label. When the format starts with '~', this '~' will only be inserted when the character before point is *not* a whitespace.

context-method

Indication on how to find the short context.

- If `nil`, use the text following the '\label{...}' macro.
- If `t`, use
  - the section heading for section labels.
  - text following the '\begin{...}' statement of environments (not a good choice for environments like eqnarray or enumerate, where one has several labels in a single environment).
  - text after the macro name (starting with the first arg) for macros.
- If an integer, use the nth argument of the macro. As a special case, 1000 means to get text after the last macro argument.
- If a string, use as regexp to search *backward* from the label. Context is then the text following the end of the match. E.g. setting this to '\\caption[[{]' will use the caption in a figure or table environment. '\\begin{eqnarray}\|\\\\' works for eqnarrays.
- If any of `caption`, `item`, `eqnarray-like`, `alignat-like`, this symbol will internally be translated into an appropriate regexp (see also the variable `reftex-default-context-regexps`).
- If a function, call this function with the name of the environment/macro as argument. On call, point will be just after the `\label` macro. The function is expected to return a suitable context string. It should throw an exception (error) when failing to find context. As an example, here is a function returning the 10 chars following the label macro as context:

```
(defun my-context-function (env-or-mac)
   (if (> (point-max) (+ 10 (point)))
       (buffer-substring (point) (+ 10 (point)))
     (error "Buffer too small")))
```

Label context is used in two ways by RefTeX: For display in the label menu, and to derive a label string. If you want to use a different method for each of these, specify them as a dotted pair. E.g. (`nil` . `t`) uses the text after the label (`nil`) for display, and text from the default position (`t`) to derive a label string. This is actually used for section labels.

magic-word-list
> List of magic words which identify a reference to be of this type. If the word before point is equal to one of these words when calling `reftex-reference`, the label list offered will be automatically restricted to labels of the correct type. If the first element of this word list is the symbol 'regexp', the strings are interpreted as regular expressions.

toc-level
> The integer level at which this environment should be added to the table of contents. See also `reftex-section-levels`. A positive value will number the entries mixed with the sectioning commands of the same level. A negative value will make unnumbered entries. Useful only for theorem-like environments which structure the document. Will be ignored for macros. When omitted or `nil`, no TOC entries will be made.

If the type indicator characters of two or more entries are the same, RefTeX will use

— the first non-`nil` format and prefix

— the magic words of all involved entries.

Any list entry may also be a symbol. If that has an association in `reftex-label-alist-builtin`, the `cddr` of that association is spliced into the list. However, builtin defaults should normally be set with the variable `reftex-default-label-alist-entries`.

reftex-section-prefixes   [User Option]
> Prefixes for section labels. When the label prefix given in an entry in `reftex-label-alist` contains '`%S`', this list is used to determine the correct prefix string depending on the current section level. The list is an alist, with each entry of the form (*key* . *prefix*). Possible keys are sectioning macro names like '`chapter`', integer section levels (as given in `reftex-section-levels`), and `t` for the default.

reftex-default-context-regexps   [User Option]
> Alist with default regular expressions for finding context. The emacs lisp form (`format regexp (regexp-quote environment)`) is used to calculate the final regular expression - so '`%s`' will be replaced with the environment or macro.

reftex-trust-label-prefix   [User Option]
> Non-`nil` means, trust the label prefix when determining label type. It is customary to use special label prefixes to distinguish different label types. The label prefixes have no syntactic meaning in LaTeX (unless special packages like fancyref) are being used. RefTeX can and by default does parse around each label to detect the correct label type, but this process can be slow when a document contains thousands of labels. If you use label prefixes consistently, you may speed up document parsing by setting this variable to a non-nil value. RefTeX will then compare the label prefix with the prefixes found in 'reftex-label-alist' and derive the correct label type in this way. Possible values for this option are:

> | `t` | This means to trust any label prefixes found. |
> | `regexp` | If a regexp, only prefixes matched by the regexp are trusted. |
> | `list` | List of accepted prefixes, as strings. The colon is part of the prefix, e.g. ("fn:" "eqn:" "item:"). |

> nil   Never trust a label prefix.

The only disadvantage of using this feature is that the label context displayed in the label selection buffer along with each label is simply some text after the label definition. This is no problem if you place labels keeping this in mind (e.g. *before* the equation, *at the beginning* of a fig/tab caption ...). Anyway, it is probably best to use the regexp or the list value types to fine-tune this feature. For example, if your document contains thousands of footnotes with labels fn:xxx, you may want to set this variable to the value `"^fn:$"` or `("fn:")`. Then RefTeX will still do extensive parsing for any non-footnote labels.

9.3 Creating Labels

reftex-insert-label-flags   [User Option]
> Flags governing label insertion. The value has the form
>
> > (*derive prompt*)
>
> If *derive* is **t**, RefTeX will try to derive a sensible label from context. A section label for example will be derived from the section heading. The conversion of the context to a valid label is governed by the specifications given in **reftex-derive-label-parameters**. If *derive* is **nil**, the default label will consist of the prefix and a unique number, like '`eq:23`'.
>
> If *prompt* is **t**, the user will be prompted for a label string. When *prompt* is **nil**, the default label will be inserted without query.
>
> So the combination of *derive* and *prompt* controls label insertion. Here is a table describing all four possibilities:
>
> | *derive* | *prompt* | *action* |
> | --- | --- | --- |
> | nil | nil | Insert simple label, like '`eq:22`' or '`sec:13`'. No query. |
> | nil | t | Prompt for label. |
> | t | nil | Derive a label from context and insert. No query. |
> | t | t | Derive a label from context, prompt for confirmation. |
>
> Each flag may be set to **t**, **nil**, or a string of label type letters indicating the label types for which it should be true. Thus, the combination may be set differently for each label type. The default settings '`"s"`' and '`"sft"`' mean: Derive section labels from headings (with confirmation). Prompt for figure and table labels. Use simple labels without confirmation for everything else.
>
> The available label types are: **s** (section), **f** (figure), **t** (table), **i** (item), **e** (equation), **n** (footnote), **N** (endnote) plus any definitions in **reftex-label-alist**.

reftex-format-label-function   [Hook]
> If non-**nil**, should be a function which produces the string to insert as a label definition. The function will be called with two arguments, the *label* and the *default-format* (usually '`\label{%s}`'). It should return the string to insert into the buffer.

reftex-string-to-label-function   [Hook]
> Function to turn an arbitrary string into a valid label. RefTeX's default function uses the variable **reftex-derive-label-parameters**.

`reftex-translate-to-ascii-function`   [Hook]

> Filter function which will process a context string before it is used to derive a label from it. The intended application is to convert ISO or Mule characters into something valid in labels. The default function `reftex-latin1-to-ascii` removes the accents from Latin-1 characters. X-Symbol (>=2.6) sets this variable to the much more general `x-symbol-translate-to-ascii`.

`reftex-derive-label-parameters`   [User Option]

> Parameters for converting a string into a label. This variable is a list of the following items:

> | | |
> |---|---|
> | *nwords* | Number of words to use. |
> | *maxchar* | Maximum number of characters in a label string. |
> | *invalid* | `nil`: Throw away any words containing characters invalid in labels.
`t`: Throw away only the invalid characters, not the whole word. |
> | *abbrev* | `nil`: Never abbreviate words.
`t`: Always abbreviate words (see `reftex-abbrev-parameters`).
`1`: Abbreviate words if necessary to shorten label string. |
> | *separator* | String separating different words in the label. |
> | *ignorewords* | List of words which should not be part of labels. |
> | *downcase* | `t`: Downcase words before putting them into the label. |

`reftex-label-illegal-re`   [User Option]

> Regexp matching characters not valid in labels.

`reftex-abbrev-parameters`   [User Option]

> Parameters for abbreviation of words. A list of four parameters.

> | | |
> |---|---|
> | *min-chars* | Minimum number of characters remaining after abbreviation. |
> | *min-kill* | Minimum number of characters to remove when abbreviating words. |
> | *before* | Character class before abbrev point in word. |
> | *after* | Character class after abbrev point in word. |

9.4 Referencing Labels

`reftex-label-menu-flags`   [User Option]

> List of flags governing the label menu makeup. The flags are:

> | | |
> |---|---|
> | *table-of-contents* | Show the labels embedded in a table of context. |
> | *section-numbers* | Include section numbers (like 4.1.3) in table of contents. |
> | *counters* | Show counters. This just numbers the labels in the menu. |

no-context
> Non-**nil** means do *not* show the short context.

follow   Follow full context in other window.

show-commented
> Show labels from regions which are commented out.

match-everywhere
> Obsolete flag.

show-files   Show begin and end of included files.

Each of these flags can be set to **t** or **nil**, or to a string of type letters indicating the label types for which it should be true. These strings work like character classes in regular expressions. Thus, setting one of the flags to '**"sf"**' makes the flag true for section and figure labels, **nil** for everything else. Setting it to '**"^sf"**' makes it the other way round.

The available label types are: **s** (section), **f** (figure), **t** (table), **i** (item), **e** (equation), **n** (footnote), plus any definitions in **reftex-label-alist**.

Most options can also be switched from the label menu itself - so if you decide here to not have a table of contents in the label menu, you can still get one interactively during selection from the label menu.

reftex-multiref-punctuation   [User Option]
> Punctuation strings for multiple references. When marking is used in the selection buffer to select several references, this variable associates the 3 marking characters '**,-+**' with prefix strings to be inserted into the buffer before the corresponding **ref** macro. This is used to string together whole reference sets, like '**eqs. 1,2,3-5,6 and 7**' in a single call to **reftex-reference**.

reftex-ref-style-alist   [User Option]
> Alist of reference styles. Each element is a list of the style name, the name of the LaTeX package associated with the style or **t** for any package, and an alist of macros where the first entry of each item is the reference macro and the second a key for selecting the macro when the macro type is being prompted for. (See also **reftex-ref-macro-prompt**.) The keys, represented as characters, have to be unique.

reftex-ref-style-default-list   [User Option]
> List of reference styles to be activated by default. The order is significant and controls the order in which macros can be cycled in the buffer for selecting a label. The entries in the list have to match the respective reference style names used in the variable **reftex-ref-style-alist**.

reftex-ref-macro-prompt   [User Option]
> Controls if **reftex-reference** prompts for the reference macro.

reftex-format-ref-function   [Hook]
> If non-**nil**, should be a function which produces the string to insert as a reference. Note that the insertion format can also be changed with **reftex-label-alist**. This hook also is used by the special commands to insert e.g. **vref** and **fref** references,

so even if you set this, your setting will be ignored by the special commands. The function will be called with three arguments, the *label*, the *default format* which normally is '`~\ref{%s}`' and the *reference style*. The function should return the string to insert into the buffer.

`reftex-level-indent`   [User Option]
Number of spaces to be used for indentation per section level.

`reftex-guess-label-type`   [User Option]
Non-`nil` means, `reftex-reference` will try to guess the label type. To do that, RefTEX will look at the word before the cursor and compare it with the magic words given in `reftex-label-alist`. When it finds a match, RefTEX will immediately offer the correct label menu - otherwise it will prompt you for a label type. If you set this variable to `nil`, RefTEX will always prompt for a label type.

`reftex-display-copied-context-hook`   [Normal Hook]
Normal Hook which is run before context is displayed anywhere. Designed for `X-Symbol`, but may have other uses as well.

`reftex-pre-refontification-functions`   [Hook]
`X-Symbol` specific hook. Probably not useful for other purposes. The functions get two arguments, the buffer from where the command started and a symbol indicating in what context the hook is called.

`reftex-select-label-mode-hook`   [Normal Hook]
Normal hook which is run when a selection buffer enters `reftex-select-label-mode`.

`reftex-select-label-map`   [Keymap]
The keymap which is active in the labels selection process (see Section 3.2 [Referencing Labels], page 9).

9.5 Creating Citations

`reftex-bibliography-commands`   [User Option]
LATEX commands which specify the BibTEX databases to use with the document.

`reftex-bibfile-ignore-regexps`   [User Option]
List of regular expressions to exclude files in `\\bibliography{..}`. File names matched by any of these regexps will not be parsed. Intended for files which contain only `@string` macro definitions and the like, which are ignored by RefTEX anyway.

`reftex-default-bibliography`   [User Option]
List of BibTEX database files which should be used if none are specified. When `reftex-citation` is called from a document with neither a '`\bibliography{...}`' statement nor a `thebibliography` environment, RefTEX will scan these files instead. Intended for using `reftex-citation` in non-LATEX files. The files will be searched along the BIBINPUTS or TEXBIB path.

`reftex-sort-bibtex-matches`   [User Option]
Sorting of the entries found in BibTEX databases by reftex-citation. Possible values:

nil	Do not sort entries.
author	Sort entries by author name.
year	Sort entries by increasing year.
reverse-year	Sort entries by decreasing year.

reftex-cite-format   [User Option]

The format of citations to be inserted into the buffer. It can be a string, an alist or a symbol. In the simplest case this is just the string '\cite{%l}', which is also the default. See the definition of `reftex-cite-format-builtin` for more complex examples.

If `reftex-cite-format` is a string, it will be used as the format. In the format, the following percent escapes will be expanded.

%l	The BibTeX label of the citation.
%a	List of author names, see also `reftex-cite-punctuation`.
%2a	Like %a, but abbreviate more than 2 authors like Jones et al.
%A	First author name only.
%e	Works like '%a', but on list of editor names. ('%2e' and '%E' work a well).

It is also possible to access all other BibTeX database fields:

%b booktitle	%c chapter	%d edition	%h howpublished
%i institution	%j journal	%k key	%m month
%n number	%o organization	%p pages	%P first page
%r address	%s school	%u publisher	%t title
%v volume	%y year		
%B booktitle, abbreviated		%T title, abbreviated	

Usually, only '%l' is needed. The other stuff is mainly for the echo area display, and for `(setq reftex-comment-citations t)`.

'%<' as a special operator kills punctuation and space around it after the string has been formatted.

A pair of square brackets indicates an optional argument, and RefTeX will prompt for the values of these arguments.

Beware that all this only works with BibTeX database files. When citations are made from the \bibitems in an explicit `thebibliography` environment, only '%l' is available.

If `reftex-cite-format` is an alist of characters and strings, the user will be prompted for a character to select one of the possible format strings.

In order to configure this variable, you can either set `reftex-cite-format` directly yourself or set it to the *symbol* of one of the predefined styles. The predefined symbols are those which have an association in the constant `reftex-cite-format-builtin`) E.g.: `(setq reftex-cite-format 'natbib)`.

reftex-format-cite-function   [Hook]

If non-**nil**, should be a function which produces the string to insert as a citation. Note that the citation format can also be changed with the variable `reftex-cite-format`. The function will be called with two arguments, the *citation-key* and the *default-format* (taken from `reftex-cite-format`). It should return the string to insert into the buffer.

`reftex-cite-prompt-optional-args`   [User Option]

> Non-`nil` means, prompt for empty optional arguments in cite macros. When an entry in `reftex-cite-format` ist given with square brackets to indicate optional arguments (for example '`\\cite[][{%l}`'), RefTeX can prompt for values. Possible values are:
>
> | | |
> |---|---|
> | `nil` | Never prompt for optional arguments |
> | `t` | Always prompt |
> | `maybe` | Prompt only if `reftex-citation` was called with C-u prefix arg |
>
> Unnecessary empty optional arguments are removed before insertion into the buffer. See `reftex-cite-cleanup-optional-args`.

`reftex-cite-cleanup-optional-args`   [User Option]

> Non-`nil` means, remove empty optional arguments from cite macros if possible.

`reftex-comment-citations`   [User Option]

> Non-`nil` means add a comment for each citation describing the full entry. The comment is formatted according to `reftex-cite-comment-format`.

`reftex-cite-comment-format`   [User Option]

> Citation format used for commented citations. Must *not* contain '`%l`'. See the variable `reftex-cite-format` for possible percent escapes.

`reftex-cite-punctuation`   [User Option]

> Punctuation for formatting of name lists in citations. This is a list of 3 strings.
>
> 1. normal names separator, like ', ' in Jones, Brown and Miller
> 2. final names separator, like ' and ' in Jones, Brown and Miller
> 3. The 'et al.' string, like ' {\it et al.}' in Jones {\it et al.}

`reftex-select-bib-mode-hook`   [Normal Hook]

> Normal hook which is run when a selection buffer enters `reftex-select-bib-mode`.

`reftex-select-bib-map`   [Keymap]

> The keymap which is active in the citation-key selection process (see Section 4.1 [Creating Citations], page 20).

`reftex-cite-key-separator`   [User Option]

> String used to separate several keys in a single '`\\cite`' macro. Per default this is '`","`' but if you often have to deal with a lot of entries and need to break the macro across several lines you might want to change it to '`", "`'.

`reftex-create-bibtex-header`   [User Option]

> Header to insert in BibTeX files generated by `reftex-create-bibtex-file`.

`reftex-create-bibtex-footer`   [User Option]

> Footer to insert in BibTeX files generated by `reftex-create-bibtex-file`.

9.6 Index Support

`reftex-support-index`   [User Option]
>   Non-`nil` means, index entries are parsed as well. Index support is resource inten-
>   sive and the internal structure holding the parsed information can become quite big.
>   Therefore it can be turned off. When this is `nil` and you execute a command which
>   requires index support, you will be asked for confirmation to turn it on and rescan
>   the document.

`reftex-index-special-chars`   [User Option]
>   List of special characters in index entries, given as strings. These correspond to the
>   `MakeIndex` keywords (*level encap actual quote escape*).

`reftex-index-macros`   [User Option]
>   List of macros which define index entries. The structure of each entry is

>   (*macro index-tag key prefix exclude repeat*)

>   *macro* is the macro. Arguments should be denoted by empty braces, as for example
>   in '`\index[]{*}`'. Use square brackets to denote optional arguments. The star marks
>   where the index key is.

>   *index-tag* is a short name of the index. '`idx`' and '`glo`' are reserved for the default
>   index and the glossary. Other indices can be defined as well. If this is an integer, the
>   Nth argument of the macro holds the index tag.

>   *key* is a character which is used to identify the macro for input with `reftex-index`.
>   '`?i`', '`?I`', and '`?g`' are reserved for default index and glossary.

>   *prefix* can be a prefix which is added to the *key* part of the index entry. If you have
>   a macro `\newcommand{\molec}[1]{#1\index{Molecules!#1}`, this prefix should be
>   '`Molecules!`'.

>   *exclude* can be a function. If this function exists and returns a non-`nil` value, the
>   index entry at point is ignored. This was implemented to support the (deprecated)
>   '`^`' and '`_`' shortcuts in the LaTeX2e `index` package.

>   *repeat*, if non-`nil`, means the index macro does not typeset the entry in the text, so
>   that the text has to be repeated outside the index macro. Needed for `reftex-index-`
>   `selection-or-word` and for indexing from the phrase buffer.

>   The final entry may also be a symbol. It must have an association in the variable
>   `reftex-index-macros-builtin` to specify the main indexing package you are using.
>   Valid values are currently

`default`	The LaTeX default - unnecessary to specify this one
`multind`	The multind.sty package
`index`	The index.sty package
`index-shortcut`	The index.sty packages with the ^ and _ shortcuts.
	Should not be used - only for old documents

Note that AUCTeX sets these things internally for RefTeX as well, so with a sufficiently new version of AUCTeX, you should not set the package here.

`reftex-index-default-macro`   [User Option]

> The default index macro for `reftex-index-selection-or-word`. This is a list with
> (*macro-key default-tag*).
>
> *macro-key* is a character identifying an index macro - see `reftex-index-macros`.
>
> *default-tag* is the tag to be used if the macro requires a *tag* argument. When this
> is `nil` and a *tag* is needed, RefTeX will ask for it. When this is the empty string
> and the TAG argument of the index macro is optional, the TAG argument will be
> omitted.

`reftex-index-default-tag`   [User Option]

> Default index tag. When working with multiple indexes, RefTeX queries for an index
> tag when creating index entries or displaying a specific index. This variable controls
> the default offered for these queries. The default can be selected with RET during
> selection or completion. Valid values of this variable are:
>
> | | |
> |---|---|
> | `nil` | Do not provide a default index |
> | `"tag"` | The default index tag given as a string, e.g. "idx" |
> | `last` | The last used index tag will be offered as default |

`reftex-index-math-format`   [User Option]

> Format of index entries when copied from inside math mode. When `reftex-index-`
> `selection-or-word` is executed inside TeX math mode, the index key copied from the
> buffer is processed with this format string through the `format` function. This can be
> used to add the math delimiters (e.g. '$') to the string. Requires the 'texmathp.el'
> library which is part of AUCTeX.

`reftex-index-phrase-file-extension`   [User Option]

> File extension for the index phrase file. This extension will be added to the base name
> of the master file.

`reftex-index-phrases-logical-and-regexp`   [User Option]

> Regexp matching the 'and' operator for index arguments in phrases file. When several
> index arguments in a phrase line are separated by this operator, each part will generate
> an index macro. So each match of the search phrase will produce *several* different
> index entries. Make sure this does no match things which are not separators. This
> logical 'and' has higher priority than the logical 'or' specified in `reftex-index-`
> `phrases-logical-or-regexp`.

`reftex-index-phrases-logical-or-regexp`   [User Option]

> Regexp matching the 'or' operator for index arguments in phrases file. When several
> index arguments in a phrase line are separated by this operator, the user will be
> asked to select one of them at each match of the search phrase. The first index arg
> will be the default. A number key *1–9* must be pressed to switch to another. Make
> sure this does no match things which are not separators. The logical 'and' specified
> in `reftex-index-phrases-logical-or-regexp` has higher priority than this logical
> 'or'.

`reftex-index-phrases-search-whole-words`   [User Option]

> Non-`nil` means phrases search will look for whole words, not subwords. This works
> by requiring word boundaries at the beginning and end of the search string. When the

search phrase already has a non-word-char at one of these points, no word boundary is required there.

`reftex-index-phrases-case-fold-search` [User Option]

Non-**nil** means, searching for index phrases will ignore case.

`reftex-index-verify-function` [User Option]

A function which is called at each match during global indexing. If the function returns nil, the current match is skipped.

`reftex-index-phrases-skip-indexed-matches` [User Option]

Non-**nil** means, skip matches which appear to be indexed already. When doing global indexing from the phrases buffer, searches for some phrases may match at places where that phrase was already indexed. In particular when indexing an already processed document again, this will even be the norm. When this variable is non-**nil**, RefTeX checks if the match is an index macro argument, or if an index macro is directly before or after the phrase. If that is the case, that match will be ignored.

`reftex-index-phrases-wrap-long-lines` [User Option]

Non-**nil** means, when indexing from the phrases buffer, wrap lines. Inserting indexing commands in a line makes the line longer - often so long that it does not fit onto the screen. When this variable is non-**nil**, newlines will be added as necessary before and/or after the indexing command to keep lines short. However, the matched text phrase and its index command will always end up on a single line.

`reftex-index-phrases-sort-prefers-entry` [User Option]

Non-**nil** means when sorting phrase lines, the explicit index entry is used. Phrase lines in the phrases buffer contain a search phrase, and sorting is normally based on these. Some phrase lines also have an explicit index argument specified. When this variable is non-**nil**, the index argument will be used for sorting.

`reftex-index-phrases-sort-in-blocks` [User Option]

Non-**nil** means, empty and comment lines separate phrase buffer into blocks. Sorting will then preserve blocks, so that lines are re-arranged only within blocks.

`reftex-index-phrases-map` [User Option]

Keymap for the Index Phrases buffer.

`reftex-index-phrases-mode-hook` [User Option]

Normal hook which is run when a buffer is put into **`reftex-index-phrases-mode`**.

`reftex-index-section-letters` [User Option]

The letters which denote sections in the index. Usually these are all capital letters. Don't use any downcase letters. Order is not significant, the index will be sorted by whatever the sort function thinks is correct. In addition to these letters, RefTeX will create a group '!' which contains all entries sorted below the lowest specified letter. In the '`*Index*`' buffer, pressing any of these capital letters or *!* will jump to that section.

`reftex-index-include-context`   [User Option]
> Non-`nil` means, display the index definition context in the '`*Index*`' buffer. This flag may also be toggled from the '`*Index*`' buffer with the `c` key.

`reftex-index-follow-mode`   [User Option]
> Non-`nil` means, point in '`*Index*`' buffer will cause other window to follow. The other window will show the corresponding part of the document. This flag can be toggled from within the '`*Index*`' buffer with the `f` key.

`reftex-index-map`   [Keymap]
> The keymap which is active in the '`*Index*`' buffer (see Chapter 5 [Index Support], page 24).

9.7 Viewing Cross-References

`reftex-view-crossref-extra`   [User Option]
> Macros which can be used for the display of cross references. This is used when 'reftex-view-crossref' is called with point in an argument of a macro. Note that crossref viewing for citations, references (both ways) and index entries is hard-coded. This variable is only to configure additional structures for which crossreference viewing can be useful. Each entry has the structure
>
> > (*macro-re search-re highlight*).
>
> *macro-re* is matched against the macro. *search-re* is the regexp used to search for cross references. '`%s`' in this regexp is replaced with the macro argument at point. *highlight* is an integer indicating which subgroup of the match should be highlighted.

`reftex-auto-view-crossref`   [User Option]
> Non-`nil` means, initially turn automatic viewing of crossref info on. Automatic viewing of crossref info normally uses the echo area. Whenever point is idle for more than `reftex-idle-time` seconds on the argument of a `\ref` or `\cite` macro, and no other message is being displayed, the echo area will display information about that cross reference. You can also set the variable to the symbol `window`. In this case a small temporary window is used for the display. This feature can be turned on and off from the menu (Ref->Options).

`reftex-idle-time`   [User Option]
> Time (secs) Emacs has to be idle before automatic crossref display or toc recentering is done.

`reftex-cite-view-format`   [User Option]
> Citation format used to display citation info in the message area. See the variable `reftex-cite-format` for possible percent escapes.

`reftex-revisit-to-echo`   [User Option]
> Non-`nil` means, automatic citation display will revisit files if necessary. When nil, citation display in echo area will only be active for cached echo strings (see `reftex-cache-cite-echo`), or for BibTeX database files which are already visited by a live associated buffers.

`reftex-cache-cite-echo` [User Option]
> Non-`nil` means, the information displayed in the echo area for cite macros (see variable `reftex-auto-view-crossref`) is cached and saved along with the parsing information. The cache survives document scans. In order to clear it, use *M-x reftex-reset-mode*.

9.8 Finding Files

`reftex-texpath-environment-variables` [User Option]
> List of specifications how to retrieve the search path for TeX files. Several entries are possible.
>
> — If an element is the name of an environment variable, its content is used.
> — If an element starts with an exclamation mark, it is used as a command to retrieve the path. A typical command with the kpathsearch library would be `"!kpsewhich -show-path=.tex"`.
> — Otherwise the element itself is interpreted as a path.
>
> Multiple directories can be separated by the system dependent `path-separator`. Directories ending in '`//`' or '`!!`' will be expanded recursively. See also `reftex-use-external-file-finders`.

`reftex-bibpath-environment-variables` [User Option]
> List of specifications how to retrieve the search path for BibTeX files. Several entries are possible.
>
> — If an element is the name of an environment variable, its content is used.
> — If an element starts with an exclamation mark, it is used as a command to retrieve the path. A typical command with the kpathsearch library would be `"!kpsewhich -show-path=.bib"`.
> — Otherwise the element itself is interpreted as a path.
>
> Multiple directories can be separated by the system dependent `path-separator`. Directories ending in '`//`' or '`!!`' will be expanded recursively. See also `reftex-use-external-file-finders`.

`reftex-file-extensions` [User Option]
> Association list with file extensions for different file types. This is a list of items, each item is like: (*type* . (*def-ext other-ext* ...))
>
> | | |
> |---|---|
> | *type*: | File type like `"bib"` or `"tex"`. |
> | *def-ext*: | The default extension for that file type, like `".tex"` or `".bib"`. |
> | *other-ext*: | Any number of other valid extensions for this file type. |
>
> When a files is searched and it does not have any of the valid extensions, we try the default extension first, and then the naked file name.

`reftex-search-unrecursed-path-first` [User Option]
> Non-`nil` means, search all specified directories before trying recursion. Thus, in a path '`.//:/tex/`', search first '`./`', then '`/tex/`', and then all subdirectories of '`./`'. If this option is `nil`, the subdirectories of '`./`' are searched before '`/tex/`'. This is

mainly for speed - most of the time the recursive path is for the system files and not for the user files. Set this to `nil` if the default makes RefTeX finding files with equal names in wrong sequence.

`reftex-use-external-file-finders`   [User Option]

Non-`nil` means, use external programs to find files. Normally, RefTeX searches the paths given in the environment variables `TEXINPUTS` and `BIBINPUTS` to find TeX files and BibTeX database files. With this option turned on, it calls an external program specified in the option `reftex-external-file-finders` instead. As a side effect, the variables `reftex-texpath-environment-variables` and `reftex-bibpath-environment-variables` will be ignored.

`reftex-external-file-finders`   [User Option]

Association list with external programs to call for finding files. Each entry is a cons cell (`type` . `program`). `type` is either `"tex"` or `"bib"`. `program` is a string containing the external program to use with any arguments. `%f` will be replaced by the name of the file to be found. Note that these commands will be executed directly, not via a shell. Only relevant when `reftex-use-external-file-finders` is non-`nil`.

9.9 Optimizations

`reftex-keep-temporary-buffers`   [User Option]
> Non-`nil` means, keep buffers created for parsing and lookup. RefTeX sometimes needs to visit files related to the current document. We distinguish files visited for
>
> PARSING Parts of a multifile document loaded when (re)-parsing the document.
>
> LOOKUP BibTeX database files and TeX files loaded to find a reference, to display label context, etc.
>
> The created buffers can be kept for later use, or be thrown away immediately after use, depending on the value of this variable:
>
> `nil`   Throw away as much as possible.
>
> `t`   Keep everything.
>
> `1`   Throw away buffers created for parsing, but keep the ones created for lookup.
>
> If a buffer is to be kept, the file is visited normally (which is potentially slow but will happen only once). If a buffer is to be thrown away, the initialization of the buffer depends upon the variable `reftex-initialize-temporary-buffers`.

`reftex-initialize-temporary-buffers`   [User Option]
> Non-`nil` means do initializations even when visiting file temporarily. When `nil`, RefTeX may turn off find-file hooks and other stuff to briefly visit a file. When `t`, the full default initializations are done (`find-file-hook` etc.). Instead of `t` or `nil`, this variable may also be a list of hook functions to do a minimal initialization.

`reftex-no-include-regexps`   [User Option]
> List of regular expressions to exclude certain input files from parsing. If the name of a file included via `\include` or `\input` is matched by any of the regular expressions in this list, that file is not parsed by RefTeX.

`reftex-enable-partial-scans`   [User Option]
> Non-`nil` means, re-parse only 1 file when asked to re-parse. Re-parsing is normally requested with a `C-u` prefix to many RefTeX commands, or with the `r` key in menus. When this option is `t` in a multifile document, we will only parse the current buffer, or the file associated with the label or section heading near point in a menu. Requesting re-parsing of an entire multifile document then requires a `C-u C-u` prefix or the capital `R` key in menus.

`reftex-save-parse-info`   [User Option]
> Non-`nil` means, save information gathered with parsing in files. The file 'MASTER.rel' in the same directory as 'MASTER.tex' is used to save the information. When this variable is `t`,
>
>   — accessing the parsing information for the first time in an editing session will read that file (if available) instead of parsing the document.
>
>   — exiting Emacs or killing a buffer in reftex-mode will cause a new version of the file to be written.

`reftex-parse-file-extension`   [User Option]
> File extension for the file in which parser information is stored. This extension is
> added to the base name of the master file.

`reftex-allow-automatic-rescan`   [User Option]
> Non-`nil` means, RefTEX may rescan the document when this seems necessary. Applies
> (currently) only in rare cases, when a new label cannot be placed with certainty into
> the internal label list.

`reftex-use-multiple-selection-buffers`   [User Option]
> Non-`nil` means use a separate selection buffer for each label type. These buffers are
> kept from one selection to the next and need not to be created for each use - so the
> menu generally comes up faster. The selection buffers will be erased (and therefore
> updated) automatically when new labels in its category are added. See the variable
> `reftex-auto-update-selection-buffers`.

`reftex-auto-update-selection-buffers`   [User Option]
> Non-`nil` means, selection buffers will be updated automatically. When a new label is
> defined with `reftex-label`, all selection buffers associated with that label category
> are emptied, in order to force an update upon next use. When `nil`, the buffers are
> left alone and have to be updated by hand, with the *g* key from the label selection
> process. The value of this variable will only have any effect when `reftex-use-`
> `multiple-selection-buffers` is non-`nil`.

9.10 Fontification

`reftex-use-fonts`   [User Option]
> Non-`nil` means, use fonts in label menu and on-the-fly help. Font-lock must be loaded
> as well to actually get fontified display. After changing this option, a rescan may be
> necessary to activate it.

`reftex-refontify-context`   [User Option]
> Non-`nil` means, re-fontify the context in the label menu with font-lock. This slightly
> slows down the creation of the label menu. It is only necessary when you definitely
> want the context fontified.
>
> This option may have 3 different values:
>
> `nil`   Never refontify.
>
> `t`   Always refontify.
>
> `1`   Refontify when necessary, e.g. with old versions of the x-symbol package.
>
> The option is ignored when `reftex-use-fonts` is `nil`.

`reftex-highlight-selection`   [User Option]
> Non-`nil` means, highlight selected text in selection and '`*toc*`' buffers. Normally,
> the text near the cursor is the *selected* text, and it is highlighted. This is the entry
> most keys in the selection and '`*toc*`' buffers act on. However, if you mainly use the
> mouse to select an item, you may find it nice to have mouse-triggered highlighting
> *instead* or *as well*. The variable may have one of these values:

nil	No highlighting.
cursor	Highlighting is cursor driven.
mouse	Highlighting is mouse driven.
both	Both cursor and mouse trigger highlighting.

Changing this variable requires to rebuild the selection and *toc* buffers to become effective (keys *g* or *r*).

`reftex-cursor-selected-face`   [User Option]
    Face name to highlight cursor selected item in toc and selection buffers. See also the variable `reftex-highlight-selection`.

`reftex-mouse-selected-face`   [User Option]
    Face name to highlight mouse selected item in toc and selection buffers. See also the variable `reftex-highlight-selection`.

`reftex-file-boundary-face`   [User Option]
    Face name for file boundaries in selection buffer.

`reftex-label-face`   [User Option]
    Face name for labels in selection buffer.

`reftex-section-heading-face`   [User Option]
    Face name for section headings in toc and selection buffers.

`reftex-toc-header-face`   [User Option]
    Face name for the header of a toc buffer.

`reftex-bib-author-face`   [User Option]
    Face name for author names in bib selection buffer.

`reftex-bib-year-face`   [User Option]
    Face name for year in bib selection buffer.

`reftex-bib-title-face`   [User Option]
    Face name for article title in bib selection buffer.

`reftex-bib-extra-face`   [User Option]
    Face name for bibliographic information in bib selection buffer.

`reftex-select-mark-face`   [User Option]
    Face name for marked entries in the selection buffers.

`reftex-index-header-face`   [User Option]
    Face name for the header of an index buffer.

`reftex-index-section-face`   [User Option]
    Face name for the start of a new letter section in the index.

`reftex-index-tag-face`   [User Option]
    Face name for index names (for multiple indices).

`reftex-index-face`   [User Option]
    Face name for index entries.

9.11 Miscellaneous

`reftex-extra-bindings`   [User Option]

> Non-nil means, make additional key bindings on startup. These extra bindings are located in the users 'C-c letter' map. See Section 7.2 [Key Bindings], page 33.

`reftex-plug-into-AUCTeX`   [User Option]

> Plug-in flags for AUCTeX interface. This variable is a list of 5 boolean flags. When a flag is non-nil, RefTeX will

> ```
>     - supply labels in new sections and environments  (flag 1)
>     - supply arguments for macros like \label         (flag 2)
>     - supply arguments for macros like \ref           (flag 3)
>     - supply arguments for macros like \cite          (flag 4)
>     - supply arguments for macros like \index         (flag 5)
> ```

> You may also set the variable itself to t or nil in order to turn all options on or off, respectively.

> Supplying labels in new sections and environments applies when creating sections with *C-c C-s* and environments with *C-c C-e*.

> Supplying macro arguments applies when you insert such a macro interactively with *C-c RET*.

> See the AUCTeX documentation for more information.

`reftex-revisit-to-follow`   [User Option]

> Non-nil means, follow-mode will revisit files if necessary. When nil, follow-mode will be suspended for stuff in unvisited files.

`reftex-allow-detached-macro-args`   [User Option]

> Non-nil means, allow arguments of macros to be detached by whitespace. When this is t, the 'aaa' in '\bbb [xxx] {aaa}' will be considered an argument of \bb. Note that this will be the case even if \bb is defined with zero or one argument.

9.12 Keymaps and Hooks

RefTeX has the usual general keymap, load hook and mode hook.

`reftex-mode-map`   [Keymap]

> The keymap for RefTeX mode.

`reftex-load-hook`   [Normal Hook]

> Normal hook which is being run when loading 'reftex.el'.

`reftex-mode-hook`   [Normal Hook]

> Normal hook which is being run when turning on RefTeX mode.

Furthermore, the four modes used for referencing labels, creating citations, the table of contents buffer and the phrases buffer have their own keymaps and mode hooks. See the respective sections. There are many more hooks which are described in the relevant sections about options for a specific part of RefTeX.

10 Changes

Here is a list of recent changes to RefTeX.

Version 4.34

- The creation of BibTeX files with `reftex-create-bibtex-file` now recognizes cross-referenced entries and '`@string`' definitions.
- RefTeX now provides better options for defining and selecting special referencing macros like '`\vref`' from the '`varioref`' package, '`\fref`' from the '`fancyref`' package or '`\autoref`' from the '`hyperref`' package as well as page-referencing macros like '`\pageref`'. See Section 3.6 [Reference Styles], page 18, for details.

Version 4.33

- Update to GPLv3.
- Parse files are created in a way that does not interfere with recentf mode.

Version 4.32

- First release by AUCTeX project.
- Installation routine rewritten after structure of source package changed.
- Activation of RefTeX changed, so make sure you read the installation instructions and remove obsolete cruft related to RefTeX from your init file.
- Fixed bug where point would end up in the wrong buffer when jumping between several LaTeX and phrases buffers.
- Fixed bug where BibTeX keys with hyphens were parsed incorrectly.
- Some performance improvements.
- The separator used between multiple citations in a \cite macro can now be changed by customizing the variable `reftex-cite-key-separator`.

Version 4.28

- Support for the Jurabib package.
- Improvements when selecting several items in a selection buffer.

Version 4.27

- Support for jurabib in 'reftex-cite-format-builtin'.
- Bug fixes.

Version 4.26

- Support for global incremental search.
- Some improvements for XEmacs compatibility.

Version 4.25

- Fixed bug with '%F' in a label prefix. Added new escapes '%m' and '%M' for mater file name and master directory.

Version 4.24

- Inserting citation commands now prompts for optional arguments when called with a prefix argument. Related new options are `reftex-cite-prompt-optional-args` and `reftex-cite-cleanup-optional-args`.

- New option `reftex-trust-label-prefix`. Configure this variable if you'd like RefTeX to base its classification of labels on prefixes. This can speed-up document parsing, but may in some cases reduce the quality of the context used by RefTeX to describe a label.

- Fixed bug in `reftex-create-bibtex-file` when `reftex-comment-citations` is non-nil.

- Fixed bugs in indexing: Case-sensitive search, quotes before and/or after words. Disabled indexing in comment lines.

Version 4.22

- New command `reftex-create-bibtex-file` to create a new database with all entries referenced in the current document.

- New keys *e* and *E* allow to produce a BibTeX database file from entries marked in a citation selection buffer.

Version 4.21

- Renaming labels from the toc buffer with key *M-%*.

Version 4.20

- Structure editing capabilities. The command keys < and > in the TOC buffer promote/demote the section at point or all sections in the current region.

- New option `reftex-toc-split-windows-fraction` to set the size of the window used by the TOC. This makes the old variable `reftex-toc-split-windows-horizontally-fraction` obsolete.

- A dedicated frame can show the TOC with the current section always automatically highlighted. The frame is created and deleted from the toc buffer with the *d* key.

Version 4.19

- New command 'reftex-toc-recenter' (*C-c -*) which shows the current section in the TOC buffer without selecting the TOC window.

- Recentering happens automatically in idle time when the option `reftex-auto-recenter-toc` is turned on.

- Fixed several bugs related to automatic cursor positioning in the TOC buffer.

- The highlight in the TOC buffer stays when the focus moves to a different window.

- New command 'reftex-goto-label'.

- Part numbers are no longer included in chapter numbers, and a new part does not reset the chapter counter. See new option `reftex-part-resets-chapter`.

Version 4.18

- `reftex-citation` uses the word before the cursor as a default search string.

- Simplified several regular expressions for speed.

- Better support for chapterbib. Different chapters can now use BibTeX or an explicit `thebibliography` environment.

Version 4.17

- The toc window can be split off horizontally. See new options `reftex-toc-split-windows-horizontally`, `reftex-toc-split-windows-horizontally-fraction`.

- It is possible to specify a function which verifies an index match during global indexing. See new option `reftex-index-verify-function`.
- The macros which input a file in LaTeX (like \input, \include) can be configured. See new option `reftex-include-file-commands`.
- The macros which specify the bibliography file (like \bibliography) can be configured. See new option `reftex-bibliography-commands`.
- The regular expression used to search for the \bibliography macro has been relaxed to allow for '{\bibliography{...}}' needed by chapterbib.
- Small bug fixes.

Version 4.15

- Fixed bug with parsing of BibTeX files, when fields contain quotes or unmatched parenthesis.
- Small bug fixes.
- Improved interaction with Emacs LaTeX mode.

Version 4.14

- Ensure write access to all files before doing global label replace.
- Fixed bug which would parse '\partial' as '\part'.

Version 4.12

- Support for 'bibentry' citation style.

Version 4.11

- Fixed bug which would parse '\Section' just like '\section'.

Version 4.10

- Renamed 'reftex-vcr.el' to 'reftex-dcr.el' because of conflict with 'reftex-vars.el' on DOS machines.
- New options `reftex-parse-file-extension` and `reftex-index-phrase-file-extension`.

[.....]

Version 1.00

- released on 7 Jan 1997.

Index

Short Contents

Table of Contents

www.ingramcontent.com/pod-product-compliance
Lightning Source LLC
LaVergne TN
LVHW060147070326

832902LV00018B/2995